From the Award Winning Author of 'Growing Up with Jessica' comes a NEW heartfelt & honest guide for 'Caregivers' & their families & friends, inspired by 37 years of real 24/7 experience.

"...after many years of 24/7 caregiving for our youngest daughter Jessica, the scales finally fell off of our eyes and we beheld the privilege we had been given as caregivers of another human soul. And finally we embraced the joy and blessings of being 'Ultimate Caregivers.'"

James Walker, Jessica's Dad & Author of
'Growing Up with Jessica: A True Story' & 'Lessons from Jessica: Ultimate Caregiving'

'Growing Up with Jessica: A True Story'
The Unexpected Parenting of a Special Needs Child.

Christian Choice Book Awards, DOUBLE Winner:

'First Place'
'Best Parenting Book'
and 1 of 3
'Grand Prize'
Winners.

"Many people look at our lives and think, 'They have taken their broken child and tried to fix her as she grew up...'

But the real truth is that Jessica 'fixed' us. Refining and improving us in many ways as we 'grew up' together. I can honestly say that our adventures in 'Jessica-land' as we unexpectedly provided care for our special needs child have changed us all for the better.

What Our Readers are saying about 'Lessons from Jessica'

"Such an inspiring book! Loved every page. Thank You!"

"I love the idea. I think it is important to let the caregiver know how much they mean to you and that they are loved."

"So very true... caregiving is a privilege."

"...an easy read that not only held my interest, but entertained me while informing and teaching me invaluable information from someone who continues to live these lessons everyday."

"Loved having the review questions to reinforce what was read..."

I enjoyed the well known examples of Viktor, Agnes, Josh, Annie & Helen, interspersed through out... it is very effective how you brought them back into the story..."

"Beautiful inspiration on JOY!"

"I want everyone to read this amazing book!"

"Intertwining your life experiences then linking them to the impact these experiences had on your life, path and choices, kept the book real and made the lessons you are sharing more profound and meaningful."

"The chapter on *'unselfish love'* ministered to me greatly..."

"...I see a readable, helpful book that needs no changes. ...I would give you an 'A' grade for the entire book, including pictures, discussion questions and appendix."

"As a *'caregiver friend'* we wish we could have read this book years ago."

"...great info on how an outsider can help & encourage. Sometimes we don't know..."

"This book is awesome!"

"Great specific, practical advice."

"I laughed with humor and joy, I was touched with empathy and emotion and I cried, sometimes in sorrow, but also I had tears of joy."

"Your book does speak to Retirement Community caregiving people."

"What a blessing to read and pour over! You once again have done a super job!"

"I liked the advice to those observing a caregiver..."

"I LOVED the ending of this book, What a beautiful and joyous picture you painted to end this story with."

"Loved the book..."

"God bless you for tackling this much needed information."

Lessons from

JESSICA:
Ultimate Caregiving

*A Longtime Caregiver's Inspirational Guide
to Understanding and Ultimately
Succeeding at Caregiving.*

by James Walker

Copyright © 2015 by James Walker
First Edition

LESSONS from JESSICA:
Ultimate Caregiving.

A Longtime Caregiver's Inspirational Guide to Understanding and Ultimately Succeeding at Caregiving.

by James Walker

Printed in the United States of America

ISBN 978-1-944080-00-6
eBook ISBN 9781944080013

All Rights Reserved solely by the author. The author guarantees all contents are original and do not infringe upon the legal rights of any other person or work. No part of this book may be reproduced in any form without the permission of the author. The views expressed in this book are not necessarily those of the publisher.

Unless otherwise indicated all Bible quotations are taken from the NIV ©1988,1989,1990,1991 by Tyndale House Publishers and the NCV © 2003 by Thomas Nelson, Inc.

www.greatnewspress.com

FAM033000-Family & Relationships : Children with Special Needs
FAM012000-Family & Relationships : Parent & Adult Child
FAM028000 Family & Relationships: Learning Disabilities

CONTENTS

Dedications

Memorial Dedication

Foreword by Pastor Harold Antrim

Notes from Jessica's Family

Chapter One, page 19
Into the UNDISCOVERED LAND
What is 'Ultimate Caregiving?'

Chapter Two, page 31
Your PROBLEMS or MINE?
A Matter of Perspective.

Chapter Three, page 39
The Glue of COMMITMENT.
A Really, Really Long Word.

Chapter Four, page 45
ENDURANCE for the RACE.
Sprint or Marathon?

Chapter Five, page 53
A LOVE that is GENUINE.
Acquiring Unselfishness.

Chapter Six, page 63
Make Lasting FRIENDSHIPS.
The Fruits of Unselfish Love.

CONTENTS   *Lessons from Jessica*

Chapter Seven, page 69
Keeping Your PERSPECTIVE.
The Width, Breadth & Depth of Life.

Chapter Eight, page 75
Developing CHARACTER.
More than a Cartoon.

Chapter Nine, page 83
Growing CONFIDENCE.
Trust in your Future.

Chapter Ten, page 89
The Miracle of HOPE.
Confidence Breeds Hope.

Chapter Eleven, page 95
Where is My PATIENCE?
Running Out of It?

Chapter Twelve, page 103
The Fruit of BLESSINGS.
Flowing From Sacrifice.

Chapter Thirteen, page 109
Amazing JOY.
Adding Everything Up.

Chapter Fourteen, page 117
Considering FAITH.
Someone is at The Door.

Chapter Fifteen, page 125
Help for HELPLESS.
Who is the Helpless One?

Chapter Sixteen, page 133
Consider the SOUL.
What is a Soul Worth?

Chapter Seventeen, page 143
It is Our PRIVILEGE.
The Greatest of them All.

Chapter Eighteen, page 151
Traveling in JESSICA-LAND.
We 'Grew Up' with Jessica.

Chapter Nineteen, page 159
Questions & Activities.
Understanding Ultimate Caregiving

The APPENDIX: page 171
Appendix: Table of Contents, page 173
Resources for Caregiving, page 175
'12 Days of Hope' Challenge, page 175
Your Review Requested, page 176
Chart of Quotes, page 177
Personal Resources, page 179
Websites & Digital Resources, page 181
Jessica Book Information 182

Lessons from JESSICA

Credits, Photo Notes Bibliographic Summary, page 185
Our Family, 'Growing Up with Jessica,' page 189
Pages for Your Personal Notes: 191-194

Dedications

This book is dedicated with love to
Jessica's big brother Jon and big sister Jamie.
Without their love, support and unselfishness
I couldn't have told this story.

And also to my wife Renée, who in my mind, is exactly
the Mother she always wanted to be.

To all of our friends who have supported us
in many, many ways over the years.
Thanks for being there in love.

A special thank you to Pastor Harold Antrim for
your consistent loving support and patience and being
the very first person to encourage me to write.
Because of you I believe I am in exactly the right place
and doing what I should be doing... at last.

And thanks to Jessica *'the blessed one'*
for all of the lessons I have learned from your
sweet influence on my body, mind and soul.

Special MEMORIAL Dedication

Special Memorial Dedication

Thanks to dear sweet Aunt Kathryn Walker and her constant encouragement to write this guide.

I especially remember during our last long talk, as I sat on the beach in Hawaii watching the waves roll in, and she sat in Villa Grove, Illinois as the snow drifted down.

A very special time of reluctant but joyful goodbyes. I will see her and Uncle Don in the 'Aloha Section.'

I also remember the excitement in her voice in our brief last talk in early June, when I told her this book was almost finished. She kept telling me how helpful she thought the 'lessons' we had learned would be to others, and then it was 'good-bye' as she was off to meet with her friends.

That was joyful Aunt Kathryn, always unselfishly thinking of the needs others.

Thanks for the inspiration.

Aloha Oé
'Farewell until we meet again.'

FOREWORD by Pastor Harold Antrim

Who would be more qualified to write about caregiving, for caregivers, than someone whose immediate family has experienced 37 years of continuous *'Ultimate Caregiving?'*

There is no one I know who has experienced so many years of *Ultimate* caregiving and is as capable of expressing it in book form more than James Walker. Also, God has given Jim a concern to help other caregivers. In Jim's words, his driving motivation is *"...to help people cope, survive and thrive when facing an overwhelming affliction such as we faced with little Jessica."*

Any parent can benefit from *'Jessica's Lessons.'*

James and Renée Walker and their children, Jamie, Jon and Jessica, are a remarkable family. Jim and Renée were active growing members of a growing church in Boise, Idaho, when I became their pastor in 1974. Their daughter Jamie Ann was six years old, their son Jon David was nearly three years old, and it would be another seven plus years before Jessica Elizabeth would be born. Their family was changed forever at the time surrounding Jessica's birth on August 25, 1978.*

In the latter part of December 1977, Renée began to experience what appeared to be morning sickness. So they went to the doctor to confirm their suspicions. The unexpected had happened. The doctor said *"...of course due to your age, and the fact that you said this was not a planned pregnancy...we could easily terminate this pregnancy."*

They both reacted immediately *"NOOO! NO, we definitely want this baby!"* They had decided. This child was going to be born and grow and prosper in their family, and they would love

Lessons from Jessica

her forever. They had made their commitment and the next August, Jessica was born – three weeks early.

Not long after her birth Jessica had some physical problems – jaundice along with daily blood tests for a time. Soon after followed baby vaccinations and having some kind of seizure activity. The doctor wasn't overly concerned, but after another DPT shot, Jessica's seizure activity increased, with jerking and twisting, going limp, etc., and it kept getting worse.

Jim & Renée knew something was terribly wrong. Jessica became completely helpless. Eventually they came to realize that Jessica might never be healed. They had hit the wall, going through the denial and anger stages, to the place of letting go in the comfort of trusting God. They discovered they could have joy & a broken heart, believing God chose them for this and accepted it as an honor from Him.

To the best they knew how, their church congregation fully supported them. But the Walker Family learned many, many lessons through the years.

Jessica was sixteen years old when I left the church in Boise and moved to Oregon to another ministry. I had gained tremendous admiration for the family and the care they gave their special daughter/sister. I have had a few times to connect with them over the past twenty years. Our most recent connection with them came July 30, 2015, when my wife and I were visiting our family in Boise. Jim had phoned me and wanted to talk with me, and since I was in town, I was delighted to arrange a time for us to visit with him and Renée.

FOREWORD

We had a wonderful extended time with them. They had let us know that through the years their lives had been changed for the better, and they would never go back on their commitment to their blessed Jessica. They told us if they had a chance to do it over, they wouldn't change it at all. They continually rejoice in their privilege of being Ultimate 24/7 caregivers for their helpless daughter, having spent the last 37 years of their lives caring for her in genuine love.

Jim brought a binder version of *'Lessons from Jessica,'* the second book he had written, and asked me to review it, which I was happy to do. I brought it with me to Oregon and reviewed it more than twice, gleaning new insights for my personal caregiving and ministry with other caregivers. I also gained more and more respect for their experiences and the commitment they kept, along with their desire to share their love and heart in order to help other caregivers.

Jim has produced a masterful book, including pictures, discussion questions and appendix. I told him if I were his teacher I would give him an 'A' grade.

My hope is that you will gain practical insights and new lessons as you read *'Lessons from Jessica: Ultimate Caregiving.'*

Pastor Harold Antrim

Pastor Antrim has spent 53 years in ministry work. Harold & his wife Marilyn have four children, seven grandchildren and five great grandchildren. December 28, 2015 marks their 65th. wedding anniversary.

* Growing Up With Jessica: A True Story. The full story of their struggles and victories over the 27 years that followed Jessica's birth was the subject of Jim's first book. Please see page 182 for more information.

Lessons from JESSICA

Notes from JESSICA'S FAMILY

Dear Reader

We have shared our heartfelt and
real life experiences in total honesty in the contents of this
caregiving guide, in a sincere effort to help other caregivers.

We do not do this for fame or fortune, but with the
realization that there are staggering numbers of
'*caregivers*' who quietly labor every single day.

Most '*caregivers*' are regular people who are facing relentless
tasks daily, sometimes against overwhelming obstacles, as they
labor to provide care for a special needs child, spouse or parent.

We are here to tell you that you can survive and
thrive if you follow the path to 'ultimate caregiving.'
That is the purpose of this caregiver's guide book.

This guide is based on our nearly four decades of
real life experience, from which we have shared
the lessons learned, as clearly and accurately as possible.

It is our sincere hope that you will receive
as big a blessing from reading this guide
as we have... as we have lived it.

*Jim & Renée
Jamie, Jon & Jessica*

Lessons from JESSICA

Into the Undiscovered Land.

Arnold Gold Photo   1984

What is Ultimate Caregiving?

Lessons from JESSICA

Chapter 1

The Undiscovered Land.

What is 'Ultimate Caregiving'

The terror of the unknown was there, waiting for us.

Renée was quietly nursing Jessica, sitting on a stool at the breakfast bar in our kitchen. It was always a very special time of closeness for her and her new baby girl.

After visiting the doctor's office and sharing our concerns about four month old Jessica's unusual behavior, we were both feeling relieved and were looking forward to the long fun New Year's holiday weekend with our family. Life was good and we were at peace, feeling safe and warm together.

I am standing at the large kitchen window watching the huge beautiful snowflakes silently drifting down to join the snowy, late December winterscape. I remember thinking how each delicate flake's existence as a totally unique little work of art was so short lived as they floated softly down into obscurity...

Suddenly without warning, Renée screamed in a frightening way that I had never heard before! Whirling around, I could see Jessica in her arms jerking and twisting violently, gasping and then suddenly going limp... her eyes half open and rolled back in her head, her skin was as white as death, and above Jessica's limp and hanging form I could see Renée's trance-like wide-eyed stare, as if to say *'This can't be happening!'*

Lessons from JESSICA

It was so quiet I remember I could hear the clock... tick... tick... ticking... in the background. Time stood still... suddenly our world had stopped turning.

Grabbing Jessica in my arms I tried to arouse her... there was no response... her head was flopping limply. I laid her on the breakfast bar and began to massage her, pinch her, poke her. She looked dead and was completely unresponsive.

I remember her skin felt strangely cold and clammy.

Continuing to work feverishly on her, I was pressing on her chest and pulling her arms up to help her breathe... time was slipping slowly by... nothing... nothing... not breathing... '*she is gone!*' I was thinking. But I couldn't stop... I wouldn't stop! '*This couldn't be happening!*'

I struggled to stay calm. Fear of the unknown... is so suffocating.

And so the terrible mystery was upon us, and our cozy little world was wobbling out of control. With a sense of foreboding we hurriedly loaded up for our second trip to the doctor's office on that fateful day... December 29, 1978.

Nothing in our family's life, would ever be the same.

Into the Undiscovered Land.

From that day forward we have lived in a different world. The world of the '*Caregiver*' or as we came to call it, '*Jessica-land.*'

We are residing there to this very day.

What is 'Ultimate Caregiving?'

Experiencing 'Jessica-land.'

After about 25 years of twists and turns and ups and downs and white knuckle roller coasters, and indescribable blessings, we were convinced by others, who had watched our journey over the years, that we should write a book about our experiences. A very emotionally hard thing to do. Another *'Jessica-land'* experience for sure.

After authoring **'Growing Up with Jessica'** and as a result, meeting and hearing from thousands of people over the years, a number of things are becoming more and more apparent.

There are many caregivers out there. I have seen estimates of over 60 million.[1] I have to wonder, who cares for them. And in addition, I am finding, almost everyone knows someone who is a caregiver.

We may find ourselves immersed without warning, into the *'land of broken toys,'* kicking and screaming as we go. There are very few places to turn for help and advice, and as mostly inexperienced non-professionals dealing with this new *'special world,'* we just don't get a lot of preparation.

We call it *'Adventures in Jessica-land.'* It is a land of many wonders. Precious moments mixed with heart throbbing terrors, but certainly not boring. It requires some *'growing up.'*

'Growing Up with Jessica'

Writing the book was very difficult. Our sole purpose for doing it, was the idea, that if just one person was comforted and helped by

Lessons from JESSICA

learning of our adventures in 'Jessica-land,' it would be worth it. Maybe they were at the threshold and would need some help and guidance. It is not easy to survive all alone. I can say today, that our hope for '*Growing Up with Jessica*' has borne fruit, at least a thousand times over!

This book, '*Lessons from Jessica*,' is created in that same spirit.

We are dedicating this guide to caregivers, and their friends and families, that they may find the blessings in their caregiving.

'Ultimate Caregiving.'

'*Ultimate Caregiving*' is when you ultimately realize the privilege of being able to set aside your own ego and selfishness, and live for that special person in your life who is helpless and afflicted. It is the ultimate form of love and a priceless blessing.

Ultimate caregiving will require choices. You must choose to love the person you are caring for unconditionally, and if you learn to embrace caregiving as a *privilege*, you will be choosing wisely.

You will be choosing to endure, and by enduring you will be developing and strengthening your character, and generating your confidence and hope for the future.

Through ultimate caregiving you will grow into the person that God desires you to become, all the while learning many precious lessons and experiencing and discovering, what I like to describe, as the '*deeper secrets of life.*'

There is no greater privilege than helping someone who is utterly

What is 'Ultimate Caregiving?'

helpless. It is the ultimate expression of the truest form of love and absolutely mirrors God's selfsame activities on our behalf.

Four types of 'Caregivers.'

Based on our many years of practical experience, meeting, observing and researching caregiving, as a full time citizen of that special world, I think it breaks down like this:

Primary: You are the caregiver.
Secondary: You are related to a primary caregiver.
Friend: You have a friend who is a primary caregiver.
Observer: You observe caregiving activities.

Each of these categories has a set of wants, needs and activities. Some are the same. Some are unique. All require choices. Some are great, some are small, but all involve some unselfish sacrifice.

Just as a successful army requires many supporters to place one soldier in the field, ultimate caregiving will happen when all of the supporters are there, doing their part. Success or failure on the front lines of caregiving depends on it.

Love in Action.

In this book you will find some different perspectives. Whether you are a mother, father, brother, sister, friend or are *'observing from afar,'* you can contribute in some caring and supporting way.

The *Appendix* contains a simple and easy, suggested action to provide support and encouragement for personal caregivers on the front lines. See *Chapter 19* for chapter study & review questions.

Lessons from JESSICA

All it takes is acquiring and applying your unselfish and loving commitment. We will share some ways that you may acquire these things. We will share with you our first hand experiences as we grew up with Jessica and how we learned to survive and learned to embrace the priviledge of caregiving and then to cherish the blessings that come from ultimate caregiving.

Unselfishness and the sacrificial form of love that is in its DNA, must be learned, it does not come naturally. You will be at the crossroads daily. Which way should you choose?

The Viktor Frankel Story.

In 1941 Young Viktor walked into his parent's kitchen and was astounded to see the answer to his prayers lying there chiseled in marble. '...Honor thy mother and father...' he read on the surface of a crumbling remanent. He knew then what he must do. He would stay and face the inevitable Nazi imprisonment of his elderly parents and perhaps eventually, even he and his young bride would be arrested.

Why is this relevant in a book about caregiving?

Because you see Viktor and his young bride, had in their hands a visa to leave Vienna and could have easily escaped to safety and a great career in the United States. Viktor chose unselfish love over self-love, and acted on it. That decision changed him forever.

He and his expectant wife were arrested and imprisoned in 1942. Over the next three years, his parents, his wife as well as his unborn child, perished in the concentration camps, but Viktor lived on to share his observations and experiences with the world, after surviving

What is 'Ultimate Caregiving?'

and ministering to his fellow inmates in the most severely trying circumstances anyone could imagine. Facing life and death and deprivation daily, upon his liberation, he wrote a book in just nine days, it was about man's search for meaning. It was a best seller, and contains many timeless observations and insights.

I believe he chose wisely, that night in his parents' kitchen.

Viktor Frankl was a prominent Jewish psychiatrist and neurologist who had distinguished himself at an early age and seemed destined for greatness. His life changed immediately when he was arrested. He survived three years of unimaginable horror, but he gained great insight into the soul of mankind in many different areas, secrets which he was able to articulate to help and care for others, for the rest of his long life.

He was able to share this comment after his liberation and release from his concentration camp experience:

> "Being human also points, and is directed, to something other than oneself. The more one forgets himself... by giving himself to a cause to serve, or another person to love... the more human he is."
> Viktor Frankel

Perhaps his ultimate eye opening realization as prisoner #119104, was forged in that crucible of human despair, that he found himself immersed in:

> "For the first time in my life I saw the truth as it is set into song by so many poets, proclaimed as the final wisdom by so many thinkers.
>
> The truth that Love is the ultimate and highest goal to which man can aspire.

Lessons from JESSICA

> *Then I grasped the meaning of the greatest secret that human poetry and human thought and belief have to impart:*
>
> *The salvation of man is through love and in love."*
>
> Viktor Frankel

Viktor Frankl was an 'ultimate caregiver' in prison, and for the rest of his life. Because of his rare combination of formal training and practical application, until his death at age 92 he ministered with love and joy, to many more generations through his books and unique insights into the human condition, than perhaps he would have ever reached, without choosing the unselfish path he traveled.

When he saw the fragment of marble that his father had managed to salvage from a syngogue, destroyed by the Nazis, he stood at a turning point in his life. He chose ultimate love. Sacrificial love.

He was willing to give up his life for another.

> *"A man who becomes conscious of the reponsibility he bears toward a human being who affectionately waits for him, or to an unfinished work, will never be able to throw away his life.*
>
> *He knows the 'why' for his existence, and will be able to bear almost any 'how.'"*
>
> Viktor Frankel

Ultimate Caregiving is a Journey.

"Jessica is having five seizures per second..." Dr. Wilson paused and looked me in the eye... "and I guess we don't know why..." His voice trailed off into an awkward silence, as we sat there holding our baby Jessica, with our hearts sinking. 'What happens now, I wondered?' That was just the first of many questions I would have, as we stumbled forward into our now uncertain future. I remember at the time feeling that a huge chasm of darkness and anxiety was before us.

What is 'Ultimate Caregiving?'

Over the years we followed many paths with very little help or guidance. We were in the wilderness without a map.

Our journey had just begun and we felt lost already.

Hope for Our Future.

As newly minted caregivers, we needed many things, but most of all we needed a reason to hope. We found it. We love to share it.

We are constantly dreaming of giving every caregiver a path to becoming an ultimate caregiver. That is why we are sharing our personal experiences and lessons, as well as the life experiences and wisdom of some notable *'hall of fame'* caregivers, that have done it.

We learned from these ultimate caregivers, who have lived long and fruitful lives, successfully putting into practice the timeless principles that we ourselves have learned to apply. Real life experiences, give us all, caregivers and care receivers alike, hope and confidence for the future and changes our *'undiscovered land'* for the better.

Experiences in Perspective.

Everyone's journey is different, everyone's journey is the same.

We all start somewhere on the pathway. Sometimes suddenly and without warning, sometimes as the inevitable result of a long term affliction. It all starts when we are facing an unsolvable obstacle that changes the course of our lives.

Now what?

Lessons from JESSICA

Your Problems or Mine?

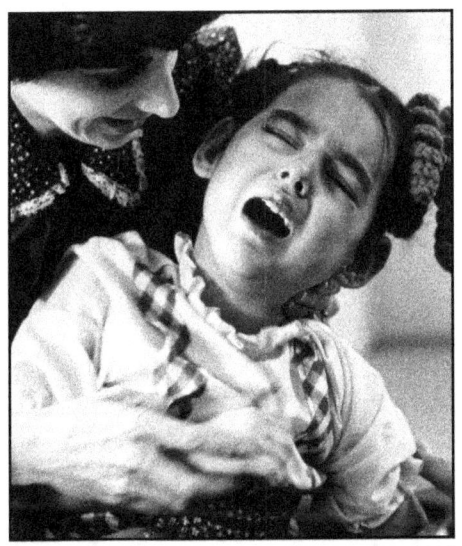

Arnold Gold Photo   1984

A Matter of Perspective.

Lessons from JESSICA

Chapter 2

Your Problems or Mine?

A Matter of Perspective.

Fred was moving and on his first Saturday in his new home, he was happily relaxing on his new overstuffed couch. Listening to the sounds of the steady rain outside, while feeling warm and snug, he was surprised to hear a knock on the door, followed by loud barking.

He answered the door and one of his new neighbors introduced himself. Inviting the man in out of the rainy weather, Fred was very surprised, as a large, wet and thoroughly muddy dog, excitedly followed close behind.

Barking gleefully the big dog quickly ran around the house leaving muddy footprints and broken lamps in his trail. Gritting his teeth and not wanting to be rude, Fred stayed calm as long as he could. But when the dog jumped up on his new sofa and began to wallow, Fred had reached the end of his patience... he snapped! Unable to keep quiet any longer, he screamed at the neighbor,

"Will you control your unruly dog? He's ruining my home!"

"My dog?" stammered the stranger, "I thought he was your dog!"

The Problem with Problems.

Our perspective is always important when it comes to dealing with daily problems. Even more so, the stubborn life-altering variety. Everyone knows that life has problems. Most of us think 'my' problems are worse than 'your' problems.

Why?

Because 'I' usually do not have to solve *'your'* problems.

Some of us of course, have an occupation that requires us to try to solve the problems of others. Police, Social Workers, Pastors, Tax Accountants, Doctors and Nurses, just to name a few.

Most caregivers are non-professionals. And based on the number of people receiving caregiving and the number of caregiving professionals available, that's the way it is and will always be.[1]

The Unchosen Path.

"*Something is wrong with Jessica...*" I heard the tears in her voice.

I was standing there looking back at Renée that crisp Halloween night. Her words were hanging in the air as the fog of her breath was rising slowly upwards into the darkness. I had no idea that a new path lay before us. We were passing a fork in the road and heading down a strange new path... here we come ready or not.

My family and I are still traveling that path. Maybe you are on a similar path right now. Maybe you will have a warning, maybe not. We had many, many questions:

'How will we survive? Why did this happen? What are the tools we will need? Where can we find them? Where does the

A Matter of Perspective

help we need come from? Will we be equal to the task? What happens next?' Needless to say, the questions can be emotionally and physically overwhelming.

We Can Survive & Thrive in Affliction.

In offering to help, we are not thinking that our problems are greater than yours. It is not the size or type of the problem that has the greatest impact. It is the location. The closer you are to the problem the greater it seems. A speck of sand in someone else's eye is not that big of a deal. However a speck of sand in your own eye... is a lot different.

After spending most of our lives, caring in love for someone who is totally helpless, we have learned some lessons. Most of them the hard way. If sharing the principles we have learned will help you or someone you know survive and thrive, then it will be worth it.

Maybe you have a friend or a relative who is a caregiver. Hopefully we can give you an insight into how to be supportive and help them in simple but tangible ways. Even a tiny act of kindness and love helps.

The Bigger Picture.

One of the secrets of coping is to see the big picture and at the same time to stay focused in the present. One day at a time. Sometimes one hour at a time. Often one minute at a time.

I will share what we have learned over the last four decades. How we went from a struggling young family with three kids to a surviving close and caring family group of eleven which now includes four grandchildren. Many people look at our lives and think, 'They have taken their broken child and tried to fix her as she grew up.'

But the real truth is that Jessica 'fixed' us. Refining and improving us in many ways as we 'grew up' together. I can honestly say that our adventures in 'Jessica-land' have changed us all for the better.

The concepts and principles I am sharing in this little book, are tested in the crucible of real experience. Most, if not all, proven in the real world of application, not just the world of theory.

We live where the 'rubber meets the road.'

We live where 'love is action.'

Common Denominators.

Also as I mentioned, I will share from a variety of other real life experiences. I will share the wisdom of others who have actually done it successfully for the long haul. Long-lived experiences of men and women, putting faith and love into action, as a caregiver or care-receiver. I began by looking for examples that reverberated with the reality of our own experiences.

I found some notable examples of lives that are woven from the threads of commitment, endurance, character, unselfish-love, friendship, patience, perspective, confidence, joy and faith.

They are examples of 'ultimate caregiving,' tested in the crucible of suffering. They stand the test of time. They all get it.

A Matter of Perspective

Perhaps by looking at the experiences of others who stood at the cross roads and chose wisely, we can learn to acquire the qualities most needed to rejoice with the tasks ahead. Even those of us who were forced to take the path less traveled, can survive and thrive.

Where to Begin.

Some wise guy would say... *"begin at the beginning..."* Okay, what is the beginning?

Some would say... *'knowledge'* some believe *'faith'* others of course say *'love.'* Maybe *'sacrifice.'* All of these are important of course and we will get into the defintions and impact of all of them as they relate to a caregiving situation, but there is something greater than and an essential part of... all of these.

Here is a hint. From the perspective of caregiving you have a problem that may be unsolvable. No quick and simple solutions. This is not a movie or a television show, this is very real, no one is riding to your rescue, it is not going away and you will be tested to the limit of your endurance... what do you need to develop?

Committment.

First, you need to be committed.

It is the word without an end... it is part of every other good thing you will need. It is your foundation. It needs to be solid rock. It is the 'glue' that will hold you and your loved ones together, as you acquire the other qualities you will need to survive and thrive.

How do you find committment?

The Undiscovered Land

Well, it helps if you are looking for it.

We were naive and inexperienced and gravitated towards it perhaps out of stubborness. We have since realized what a critical factor that was and what a lesson we were learning by making our commitment. That choice has played into the events that followed, over and over again.

Why is commitment so critical for *'ultimate caregiving?'*

The Glue of Commitment.

Arnold Gold Photo   1984

A Really, Really Long Word.

Lessons from JESSICA

Chapter 3

The 'Glue' of Commitment.

A Really, Really Long Word.

It was very quiet in the examination room where we sat with Jessica. My heart was thumping out of my chest.

After what seemed like an eternity, the doctor cleared his throat, *"...uhmmm, well you know, Jessica is very young and... well, babies do some funny things..."* He stood and moved toward the door with a shrug, *"...it's most likely nothing to be concerned about,"* he said, continuing toward the door, reaching for the knob.

At that moment, I was replaying everything in my mind... Renée's terrifying scream... the jerking... the paleness... the white's of Jessica's eyes showing through her half open eyelids... the smell of death. The desperation in my heart.

I stepped in front of the doctor and shut the door. Our eyes met.

Where to Begin.

When you are facing the unknown, which probably includes a bewildering affliction, such as we found ourselves eye to eye with, you begin to fully understand what *'commitment'* means.

Commitment is the word without an end. It is a critical part of every other good thing. It is easy to say, but hard to do. It requires that you choose it and it requires sacrifice. Two things that do not come naturally or easily. That is why deep commitment is rare.

Choosing to Commit.

Why is commitment so difficult? When we look around us in the world today it is easy to see *'lack of commitment.'* A case can be made that lack of commitment leads to many secondary problems.

As caregivers our commitment is tested everyday. We are tested in every way imaginable and in ways we cannot imagine. We have to get in the fight and get our hands dirty. With commitment firmly chosen we will get up when we are knocked down, we will keep going when we are tired, we will never stop trying to succeed.

It is the glue we need to hold things together. I believe it is a very critical difference maker. Consider this:

> *What is faith without commitment?*
>
> *What is love without commitment?*
>
> *What is friendship without commitment?*
>
> *What is a relationship without commitment?*
>
> *What is hope without commitment?*
>
> *What is confidence without commitment?*
>
> *What is joy without commitment?*
>
> *What is a caregiver without commitment?*
>
> *Who am I without commitment?*

A Really, Really Long Word

Choose 'Ultimate' Commitment.

The legendary football coach Vince Lombardi, once said,

> *"...fatigue makes cowards of us all."*
> Vince Lombardi

Why did he say that?

I suspect he was looking for a greater commitment from his players. He wanted them to work hard in the weight room and improve their conditioning, far from the adoring crowds.

He got it.

If you are committed you will make better choices. And those choices will augment your commitment. We all have a free will. Our will is something we all struggle to control. Sometimes we do the very things we shouldn't. We have that second piece of pie. We skip our exercise. We drive too fast. And the list goes on.

To make an *'ultimate commitment'* as a caregiver, is very hard. We hesitate because we know it involves... work! And with the kind of deep commitment needed, there is no going back. Seriously, there is nothing wishy-washy about the kind of commitment we are looking for here.

Ultimate commitment will make the difference in our journey.

You must choose to commit yourself to the afflicted person, whether it be your spouse, your friend or in our case our baby girl. You are committing to never leave them or forsake them. To never give up on them... ever. Body, mind and soul... committed.

Lessons from JESSICA

A Personal Decision?

Yes. Each one of us must make that personal choice. It is like links in a chain. The strongest chain has no weak links.

You can not fake it... forever. Sooner or later a superficial commitment will run out of gas. Without commitment we are riding for a fall. You can expect trouble in all of your love-based relationships. Commitment opens the door to greater things.

Being a caregiver can and will disrupt your marriage, if you are not both individually committed. A group or a family can also be committed and that is okay, but it will only be as committed as the least committed person.

Fueling Your Commitment.

Building on your foundation of commitment is absolutely a necessity. Once you have committed your heart and mind and soul to the task at hand you are ready to move forward. You have the potential to survive, and even thrive, in the heart of the storm.

You can do it if you are stubborn in your love. Someone who may be helpless to survive without you will need exactly that.

When you add a very special kind of unselfish love, you add more dimensions to your caregiving. You have added meaning and the will to endure anything, for the one you love and care for. A special kind of endurance is the result.

That is the first fruit of commitment.

Endurance for the Race.

Arnold Gold Photo 1984

Sprint or Marathon?

Lessons from JESSICA

Chapter 4

Endurance for the Race.

Sprint or Marathon?

I touched Jessica's cheek. She was on fire and laboring to breathe.

I placed her on the car seat next to me where I could reach out and feel her little chest. I could feel it moving ever so slightly. I slammed the car into gear and raced at top speed toward the hospital.

Fortunately, it was down a main street, only about five miles from our house. No time for caution.

It was late at night and there was very little traffic, so I didn't hold anything back, as I roared down the street. I remember catching my breath as I listened to Jessica's ragged, gasping and wheezing. Then silence. I pressed on her chest. The gasping resumed.

I screeched to a halt in the glare of the emergency room lights. I could see the staff running to meet me. As I was racing there, they obviously had received Renée's desperate phone call, and were ready.

I had raced against time... but I wondered... was I quick enough?

Staying in the Race.

Sometimes speed is needed. But more often than not, as a caregiver, you need to just stay in the race and stumble forward.

Lessons from JESSICA

Legend has it that the very first marathoner died from the effort. Hmm... not a happy thought, but evidently true. As caregivers, we must survive and race again and again and again. We will fall but we must get up again.

That is the first fruit of commitment. That is endurance. The bottom line is you just keep going, when you don't feel like it or even want to.

We Endure Because we are Committed.

Endurance is one of those fruits of commitment that bridges the gap between 'theory' and 'application.' If you are committed to helping the helpless, afflicted person in your life, and you love them unselfishly, you will love them more than yourself. You will be willing to give up everything for them, even life itself. You refuse to surrender to circumstances. You will not stop until the end.

As Viktor Frankel concluded after his horrific prison experience.

> *"He knows the 'why' for his existence, and will be able to bear almost any 'how.'"*
>
> Victor Frankel

Your ultimate commitment of love, enables you to endure.

Down but Not Out.

Sometimes you will be knocked flat.

Sometimes you may feel crushed and alone. You will have your failures. I remember locking myself in my office and needing to be coaxed out. You only fail if you stay down. Sometimes you need a hand up. This is where a friend or observer can help through encouragement and empathy. A simple note slipped under the door. A small encouraging card in the mail. A smile.

Small acts of kindness are not really that small. As a friend, relative or an observer, the effort it takes is very small. But amazing things can happen when you put your love and concern into action.

When we published *Growing Up with Jessica* many of our friends and acquaintances were shocked to discover the perils, trials and tribulations, and the trauma, we had experienced over the years. Sometimes on a daily basis.

We heard a lot of comments like,

"...we had no idea..." or "...wish we would have known..." or how about this one, "...call if you need anything..."

Well, we all do it, don't we?

In all of that time we were struggling to stumble forward, we received some encouragement but not on a regular visible basis. We received maybe a dozen or so cards of support for instance, and we treasured everyone of them. I am talking about people we knew and saw regularly.

Why is this kind of thing happening?

I am sure it is not because they didn't care. I am sure they cared. I am sure they prayed for us and were concerned. So what is happening here? I think I have some insights and ideas to help.

Lessons from JESSICA

Unselfish Love *is* Action.

Sometimes we ignore the elephant in the room. It is not that our friends and relatives do not care, it is more a case of not knowing what to do. I believe that most people are touched and do care.

There is a certain awkwardness that comes over us when we are exposed to those who are afflicted, and their caregivers. I would say life in *'Jessica-land'* is frightening to them. So they freeze up.

As others observe your life as a caregiver, or you share with them, they feel unsure of what to do or how to do it. For a number of reasons.

It is probably outside of their circle of confidence.

They feel awkward and unqualified.

And maybe most of all, another factor I believe, is perspective. They don't realize that even the smallest kindness can brighten your day. You don't need the marines to send in a chopper and rescue you. You may only need a smile or a kind word, or maybe just someone to take out the garbage.

Think of the caregivers you know. Should you wait until they *'call for help?'* Or just do something... anything... now? Remember you can take the *'speck'* out of their eye and it is easy.

Trust me. They all need some help and encouragement whether they are asking or not. Start small and you will be pleasantly surprised. As caregivers we may just be too shy, too proud, or just too overwhelmed to ask for help. Don't be afraid to act.

Sprint or Marathon?

I don't doubt for a second that our friends stand behind us and will be there in many ways. Sometimes we just don't share our pain. We need to be doing that more. Great blessings are waiting.

A small act of kindness speaks volumes. It is not necessary to do something big to be supportive. An act of unselfish love is like an air freshener in a stuffy room. It expands to affect the entire room.

The 'Cinderella Man.'

One of my favorite movies is the true story of James J. Braddock, a down on his luck 'depression era' boxer. At one point in his career he was injured and turned to working on the docks. He had to beg for money to feed his family & get the heat turned back on.

Through his commitment to his family he endured the tough times and got a second chance and eventually became World Heavy Weight Boxing Champion.

In his title bout he is knocked down, but gets up to win the fight.

It is a great story of love and redemption. When reporters asked him before his title fight why he would get in the ring with the undefeated Max Baer, who had fatally injured a number of opponents, he thought of his hungry children and replied, "*For Milk!*"

That is the heart and soul of commitment and endurance. You are doing it for someone who may be helpless and most likely cannot help themselves, and you love them *more* than yourself. Your love and commitment makes you get back up and battle on.

Lessons from JESSICA

Enduring to the Finish.

This is not easy. You will not always *feel* like *'enduring.'* You will fail at times and be driven to your knees, over and over. Sometimes barely hanging on.

When you feel like quitting just spend some time alone with the object of your caregiving. Watch them sleep and see them dream.

No matter what, if you love them and are committed to their care, you will be inspired to go on. You will be enduring.

You will be doing it for them.

A Love that is Genuine.

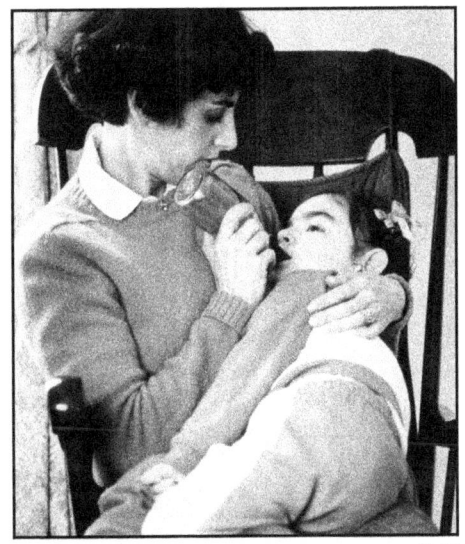

Arnold Gold Photo   1984

Acquiring Unselfishness.

Lessons from JESSICA

Chapter 5

A Love that is Genuine.

Acquiring Unselfishness.

August 26, 1910 in Skopje, Macedonia a baby girl was born.

The next day her parents named her Agnes. As young Agnes grew up in her faith, she learned the value of making a commitment, later she learned endurance through years of service.

Through her commitment and endurance she fully embraced unselfish love. Realizing what true unselfish love was, she took action. As she responded in this way she reflected the love and compassion of God, and Agnes changed the world.

And when she died, Agnes Gonxhe Bojaxhiu was one of the most revered figures in history. Everyone knew her as Mother Teresa.

In 1979 she received the Nobel Peace Prize and in her acceptance speech she shared this story of her experiences when visiting a 'retirement' home.

"...and I went there, and I saw in that home that they had everything, beautiful things, but everybody was looking towards the door. And I did not see a single one with their smile on their face...

...and I turned to the Sister and I asked... 'How is that?'

Lessons from JESSICA

"...and she said, 'This is nearly every day, they are expecting, they are hoping that a son or daughter will come to visit them. They are hurt because they are forgotten.'

"...and see this is where love comes... that poverty comes right there in our own home, even neglect to love. Maybe in our own family we have somebody who is feeling lonely, who is feeling sick, who is feeling worried... are we there, are we there to receive them?"

Mother Teresa

Mother Teresa did not make 'unselfish love' great. As she gave herself over to it, 'unselfish love' made her the great embodiment of love that is evidenced in her life. She turned theory into action.

The Love Decision.

If the most profound form of love is *'unselfish'* then the polar opposite of that would be *'selfish'* or self-love. Everywhere we look it is easy to find this kind of love.

Self-love is a state of heart, mind and soul where promotion and focus of self interest, comfort or pleasure is the primary motivation. You are the center of the universe. Sound familiar?

Self-love comes naturally and is the opposite of the kind of world altering love, that can change an Agnes into a Mother Teresa.

Unselfish love is a choice. Unselfish love is a decision. Unselfish love embodies the unconditional commitment of your soul.

Unselfish love says, '...I love you now and forever regardless of the way you look, the way you think, the way you behave or

Acquiring Unselfishness

even your response to my love. I will lay down my life for you in a heartbeat. I will never stop loving you and nothing can separate me from my love for you.'

Ultimate Love & Caregiving.

The good news is that kind of 'ultimate love' is available to all of us. We do not have to change the world or do enormous things.

> "Not all of us can do great things.
> But we can do small things with great love."
> Mother Teresa

As caregivers this ultimate love makes us realize what a privilege it is to care for the helpless. It is the greatest power in the universe.

Josh is in the Building.

When I wrote '*Growing Up with Jessica*,' just as I finished the first draft, I heard on the radio that Josh McDowell, the world famous Christian author and speaker, was coming to my hometown, that very week. Josh has had a profound impact on my life and our family. In fact, I give him credit in the book, and recommend his writings to those honestly seeking answers for their own personal decisions about God.

Since I had included him in the book I thought perhaps the proper protocol would be to present a copy to him and get his reaction, good or bad. It was not too late to change the book if he did not want to be mentioned or associated with it.

I had attended a few of his lectures and knew that he would come

Lessons from JESSICA

out and greet the audience before he spoke. If I was there, I might have the opportunity to speak to him about it.

Here is What Happened.

As I was driving to the meeting at a church not far from my house, I was plagued with doubts. *'He won't have time for me,'* I mused *'...this is a dumb idea!'* When I arrived, the place was packed and the only seat left was right in the front row on the aisle.

As I sat there I was once again filled with doubt. I turned and looked cautiously down the aisle... There comes Josh striding my way looking me right in the eye and smiling. For a moment I froze.

Standing up, I turned in his direction. I was holding in my arms the *'Growing Up with Jessica'* manuscript, .

On the cover of the notebook was a photo of Jessica. We shook hands and as I was introducing myself, and he was reaching for it, he asked me, *"...who is the beautiful girl in the photo."* I handed it to him and mumbled something about my little girl Jessica.

He scanned the manuscript inside the notebook and asked me, *"Jim would you do me a favor..."* pausing and looking me in the eye, *"Could I borrow this and read it?"* I was stunned. *"Sure..."* I mumbled. Remember, that was why I was there. Amazing.

"Here is my personal cell phone number," Josh said excitedly, *"...I will be at a family gathering in Europe in three weeks, call me and I will let you know what I think."* I was stunned into utter and complete silence. I shook my head, yes. I finally spoke, *"Yes!"*

Acquiring Unselfishness

Unselfish Love Transforms.

Imagine if you will, a young boy of twelve, tying his alcoholic father up and trying to poison him, who later in life was saying with love and compassion to that very same father, *"...Dad, I love you."*

Imagine a brilliant, young, agnostic college student, who went from ridiculing and berating Christianity, to becoming one of the world's most influential defenders of the Christian faith.

Imagine an abusive family where neither parent went beyond the second grade and their son becoming the author of 142 books.

That is the story of Josh McDowell. Unselfish love changed him.

I had heard his testimony quite a few times and it is dramatic. But the thing I remember most is watching him, months after our first encounter. I returned to meet with Josh after making the phone call he asked for, and talking with him about my book project. He was enthusiastic and encouraging.

We had arranged to meet after his next meeting in Boise. Once again the place was packed except for two seats in the front row. I sit down and a few minutes later, here comes Josh out of the blue and sits next to me. Amazing.

The meeting was to promote a series of youth meetings. At the end Josh offered free tickets to any parent who was there and couldn't afford it. A huge crowd responded. Since I was supposed to meet with him later, I was standing close by and saw him talking and greeting parents and young people who had responded. I will never forget the loving and caring he radiated.

Lessons from JESSICA

Riding the Rails.

Welcome to the caregiving roller coaster. You will notice there are three rails on this wild and crazy, caregiving ride.

Commitment... get on board.

Endurance... hang on tight.

Unselfish Love... the third rail. Where the inexhaustible supply of power is coming from. This is the power that fuels commitment. This is the power that keeps you moving forward when you think your endurance is gone. This is the power that will keep you getting up for one more round, for the loving care of someone.

Why Not Love?

Why do I focus on *commitment* first? Why not *love*?

Because *'unselfish love'* is in the DNA of *'commitment'* and that produces an *'ultimate commitment,'* and that enables us to generate the endurance we are needing for the task at hand.

A True Decision.

The bottom line is you must make a commitment to acquire the *'unselfish'* part of unselfish love. This kind of earth changing, life changing love, is a decision. A true decision requires commitment.

A true decision says, '...I am committed to love you and care for you until the very end because I love you *more* than I love myself.'

Acquiring Unselfishness

A Love that is Genuine.

Unselfish love is 'genuine' love in the sense that it is the real deal.

I am not saying that other forms of love do not exist. I am saying that our experiences and the experiences of others, like Agnes and Josh and Viktor, have validated the necessity for the infinite depth and breadth, of such a life changing and world changing love.

We all experience other forms of love. But I believe that if we are to survive and thrive as caregivers, we need the ultimate form of love in our hearts.

> *"For the first time in my life I saw the truth...*
> *...The salvation of man is in love and through love."*
>
> Viktor Frankel
> Concentration Camp Survivor
> Author, Psychiatrist & Speaker

> *"...True love is spelled g-i-v-e. It is not based on what you can get, but rooted in what you can give to the other person."*
>
> Josh McDowell
> Former Agnostic Critic of Christianity
> Author & Speaker

> *"Do not think that love in order to be genuine has to be extraordinary. What we need is to love without getting tired. Be faithful in small things..."*
>
> Mother Teresa
> Founder of Missionaries of Charity of Calcutta

Lessons from JESSICA

Make Lasting FRIENDSHIPS.

Renée & Dear Friend Linda — 2014

The Fruits of Unselfish Love.

Lessons from JESSICA

Chapter 6

Make Lasting Friendships.

The Fruits of Unselfish Love.

We walked past the warm smell of popcorn out into the balmy August night. I glanced up and saw a large banner stretched across the entire theater walk-way, it said something like, 'Happy 50th...'

As I spun slowly around to look behind me, I said "Hey look... someones getting a big surprise!" Suddenly I noticed everyone was looking at us. When I turned back around they had dropped the banner and behind it sat a smoothly purring stretch limo.

The surprise 50th birthday party for Renée and Jim was on!

I don't know if you have ever been surprised with a party but you never get over it. Imagine experiencing an ambush, of course without the bullets. In our family it is something we love to do. I surprised Renée on her 18th birthday. And also on her 21st, 30th & 40th birthdays. It is a Walker tradition we love.

We were driven aimlessly around for quite a while, enjoying treats in the limo, and then blindfolded and taken to a secret location, which turned out to be our own backyard. When we removed the blindfolds we were very surprised to see a luau in full swing complete with a live hawaiian band and at least 50 of our friends.

Later we were given an *'all expenses paid'* vacation to Maui. Wow.

Lessons from JESSICA

Friendships.

See what I mean? It's the little things that count. Wow.

Seriously though, you cannot overestimate the value of having the support of genuine friends. You know who they are, the friends who know all your faults and love you anyway. They are more precious than gold. They are life-long friends.

Our big birthday surprise was an exceptional experience. It is a memory we are still treasuring today. The trip was also the first time of separation from Jessica in about 17 years. Our kids took over and cared for her so that we could enjoy our trip to the max.

Genuine friendships are a really critical part of caring for a caregiver. They usually are made up of closer friends and relatives. They make your life bearable when it seems unbearable.

But you do not need to be in this category to make a big difference. Don't be afraid to befriend a caregiver. They may not ask for your friendship but trust me they will appreciate the smallest kindness.

A smile. A hug. A card in the mail. A *'small thing done with great love'* as Agnes said, can make their day. You don't have to save them from all their troubles or make all of their problems go away. It is enough, to be their caring friend. You can be that friend.

Caregiver Isolation.

"Hi Jim... *we are heading to the movies tonight,*" the voice said, "*...would you and Renée like to join us.*" I look at the clock. Its almost 6:30 pm, Jessica's dinner time. Doing anything that

The Fruits of Unselfish Love.

spontaneous is pretty much out of the question, " *No... I am sorry, we can't make it...*" I mumble, feeling disappointed.

"*Okay maybe next time...*"

"*Sure, maybe next time...*" I slowly hang up, and I am thinking... '*I hope so...*' as another fun opportunity fades away.

On the other end they are thinking, '*Walker's have a lot of serious responsibility, we probably shouldn't be bugging them.*'

Why are friendships so important for caregivers?

There is a process that occurs when you are a caregiver. I like to call it '*isolation by default.*' No caregiver sets out to be isolated. No friend or relative sets out to be isolated from a caregiver. It happens very slowly and almost imperceptibly over time.

As a caregiver you are in a different mode. You are focused on meeting the needs of another person. Meeting their needs before your own. Meeting the needs of someone who may be helpless.

It presents a difficult situation. A situation that typically is remaining unresolved. As caregivers we find ourselves farther and farther from the mainstream of normal activities, and sometimes, others see our lack of participation, as an act of rejection. It's not.

Be a Friend, Make a Friend.

Please understand this is not about self pity. We need friendships and support more than ever. Sometimes we are too shy or too busy or too stressed to seek friendships. Sometimes observers or

Lessons from JESSICA

friends or relatives are too shy or too uncomfortable in our world. Perhaps it is a feeling that we are too obligated to have the time.

And so those of us who need friendships in the worse way, and those of us whose heart may ache to offer friendship, remain apart.

One of the purposes of this book is to try to bridge that gap.

I will admit it is hard for me to write this down. It is a feeling of self-conviction for my own personal lack of outreach, and maybe a certain amount of pride and insensitivity over the years, to the friendly overtures of other people. A form of tunnel vision.

I have also been on the other side of the coin. That was before little Jessica came along and we started dwelling in a new and different land. A land where angels of love and mercy, and giants of crushing hurt and despair, are roaming freely. My eyes are open now. Jessica changed me for the better.

Offer Your Friendship.

I sincerely hope you will be encouraged to befriend, or be a closer friend, with a caregiver you know or see. Don't be afraid.

If you are a caregiver don't be afraid to make your needs known. Don't cry alone. Keep your perspective. Try to see your unselfish commitment and enduring love for a helpless one, as a *blessing* and a *privilege*. It is the steady pathway to overcoming your burdens and embracing the mission ahead.

Together we will bear our burdens and we will be blessed.

Keeping Your PERSPECTIVE.

Arnold Gold Photo   1984

The Width, Breadth & Depth of Life.

Lessons from JESSICA

Chapter 7

Keeping Your Perspective.

The Width, Breadth & Depth of Life.

I was watching Jessica calmly sleeping in the bowels of the massive CAT Scan machine. It clicked and whirred, as it moved her in tiny increments, slowly and methodically along the bed of the machine. After each movement it stopped and snapped a 360 degree x-ray of her brain, producing in thin slices, astounding images of the inside of her head.

She looked so sweet and delicate lying there in her little lacey pink dress and patent leather shoes. The lighted red cross-hair on her forehead, brought stark reality, to the serenity of that moment.

I remember thinking that we would have a long road ahead of us. *'Maybe this is as good as it gets,'* I thought... *' maybe she will never recover.'* I looked up. Renée was watching, looking scared.

As she watched her heart sank lower and lower with each 'click' and 'whir' of the machine. *'This can't be happening,'* she was thinking... *'we will find a cure and make Jessica whole again and everything will be back to normal.'* She was desperate for that cure and in her mind and heart, that was the only option.

"Nothing remarkable to report..." the Doctor said with little emotion, "nothing." The CAT Scan was normal.

'I can not go on like this,' Renée was thinking '...I can't stand it.'

Lessons from JESSICA

The Power of Perspectives.

Something that Renée and I had never even given a thought to, was about to rear it's head... the power of perspectives. What?

There is another seldom used phrase that describes the dilemna of different perspectives. It is *'Paradigm Shift.'* Here is an example.

Imagine you are on foot, walking across the desert.

As you are walking you are thinking of one thing... food. Not just any food, but a big thick steak with all the trimmings. As you stagger up the next hill you smell something cooking. The smell of steaks cooking on a barbecue. Smells heavenly.

Your mouth begins to water, as you stumble over the top of the hill and spot a roadside diner just ahead. As you approach, the smell of barbecueing steaks overpowers your senses.

You enter and slump in a booth. Everywhere you look you see delicious looking thick steaks being eaten. You order a steak without even looking at the menu.

You wait in painful anticipation. At last here comes your steak. As the waiter places it in front of you he says...

"Did you know that all of our steaks are 100% horse meat?"

Suddenly you lose your appetite. That is a paradigm shift.

When your long and short term hopes and dreams are altered unexpectedly, it is time to find a hand-hold and hold on tight.

The Width, Breadth & Depth

Getting Your Grip.

We need to understand as caregivers that perspective is an issue. It is an issue that, if ignored, will affect your attitude, your morale, empathy and your understanding. Perspective is a big part of life.

In the early years, I had vastly underestimated the power that our different perspectives would play, as we struggled to deal with the future of our family. Perspective is a thing that we must bring under control. I believe that we can. It is like love. We *can* decide.

We always hear the *'...glass half empty or half full...'* Being optimistic or pessimistic is really about perspective. Also feeling hopeless or hopeful is really about our perspective.

In our close, caregiving family, we must find a shared perspective. We need to all be looking at a target and it needs to be the same target... the same bullseye. However we may each be firing different kinds of primary ammo.

I am firing protection and leadership and enabling. Renée is firing tenderness and nurturing and grooming and empathy. We overlap and we share, we are the same in our goals but seek them in different and distinct ways. The shared perspective of a team.

One Day at a Time.

It is a very powerful aid to have an optimistic perspective for the future, but it is important to live it one day at a time. As our little friend Agnes commented, *"Yesterday is gone, tomorrow is not here. We have today. So let us begin."* We need to understand as caregivers that *'perspective'* is a very important issue.

Lessons from JESSICA

Choosing Your Perspective.

I mentioned at the start that after nearly 40 years of living in the caregiving world, I am seeing basically four categories:

Primary: You are the caregiver.
Secondary: You are related to a primary caregiver.
Friend: You have a friend who is a primary caregiver.
Observer: You observe caregiving activities.

Those four types of experiences are really, at least initially, defined by our perspective. By our free choice we can move from *Observer* to *Friend* and then of course our perspective changes.

As the *Primary* or *Secondary* caregiver your perspective can change from optimistic and hopeful to pessimistic and despondent and back again... depending on your day to day perspective.

We can really only think one thought at a time. Keeping our perspectives on the level and focusing on the positive is by its very nature... a conscious choice. As we choose we can have a better perspective. We can look forward to each day. One at a time.

It is possible to have joy with a broken heart... with the right perspective. I experience it everyday. I also believe that only God can turn evil into good. Choices change our perspective.

I also confess that we do not all look to God or even believe. That is a perspective that results from our choices in life. We all have a free will. If we use our free will to choose wisely, our perspectives will change for the better. I know because I have experienced it.

Developing CHARACTER.

Arnold Gold Photo   1984

More Than a Cartoon.

Lessons from JESSICA

Chapter 8

Developing CHARACTER.

More Than a Cartoon.

Albert was born near the French border in a little, obscure village in Germany. The year was 1875 and the new century and the 'world at war,' was yet to come. Growing up under the guidance of his father's church, he was exposed to fine music every day.

Little Al showed a great aptitude and innate musical ability in general, and specifically in playing the organ, so gifted in fact, that he was tutored and trained free, by the best professionals.

He rose quickly in stature and talent. By the age of 29, he had become the holder of multiple degrees and prominent university and musical appointments. His life path seemed set, his future secure as a performer, theologian, philosopher and author.

His organ concerts received rave reviews and were well attended. His books were widely acclaimed. The world was at his feet.

One day as he was reading a *Paris Missionary Society's* news publication, he saw an urgent appeal for physicians in the French colony of Gabon, deep in the heart of Africa. Finishing the article, he knew that his search for his life's work was over. He saw his future before him and the life-changes he would be embracing.

He soon announced his intentions. His family, his fans and musical supporters, his employers and associates were horrified.

Lessons from JESSICA

Albert resigned his positions, his lectures and his concerts. He had decided to enroll in a grueling seven year medical curriculum and become a missionary doctor, even though he had no experience.

He received his medical degree with a specialization in tropical medicine at the age of 38. He then applied to the original organization that had inspired him to make this dramatic change, the *Paris Missionary Society*... they turned him down flat!

What would Albert Schweitzer do now?

Developing Character.

Character is like the rudder or steering on a ship. With it you can set a course... you may hit some waves or even some rocks but without it you will drift at the whim of the wind and tides. Never a good idea for the long term, if you want to survive.

Where does chararacter come from? Well, it is an acquired asset. It is more of a habit. As we choose to love, and as we choose our personal perspectives, more choices constantly present themselves.

For instance, as we choose wisely, we learn how we should go. Repeat honesty, courage, integrity, unselfish love, sacrificial caregiving, demonstrate commitment, practice endurance, etc. Eventually these things become a part of our make up and become more instinctive. Good choices lead to more good choices.

It is the real you or me.

Commitment, endurance and unselfish love are the best foundation for our character. A strong foundation is needed.

Good Character Grows in Adversity.

Good character doesn't just happen. Bad character doesn't just happen. If good character has unselfish love, commitment and endurance in its DNA then the opposite would be an unstable, surrender to selfishness. Seems easier and probably is, but usually ends in disaster, for us and those around us.

Good Character Overcomes Circumstances.

Albert faced seven years of scorn and scolding from most of those he loved. Then he faced the shocking rejection of the very group that he had dedicated himself to helping.

His response was to continue unabated toward his higher calling in spite of the circumstances. He went out and raised his support for two years with the help of his wife who was a trained nurse.

In March of 1913, Mr. & Mrs. Albert Schweitzer left for Africa and the French Congo. They began their health care hospital in a former chicken coop, eventually adding new buildings and treating thousands of native Africans. Many of his grateful patients traveled long distances to receive great care with great love.

In 1953, Dr. Albert Schweitzer at the age of 78, was honored by the Nobel Peace Prize for his humanitarian work. He died at his beloved hospital in Africa on September 4, 1965 at the age of 90.

Little Albert had changed the world through his strength of character. He learned that adversity and circumstances could not defeat him. Delaying him was not defeat. He stayed true to his principles. He became a man of strong and good character.

Lessons from JESSICA

Character and Caregiving.

Interesting to me that at about a year before Albert lay dying in Africa, I was sitting in my '57 Volkswagen at Julia Davis Park with Renée by my side. I had a diamond engagement ring in my pocket.

She said 'yes' that afternoon, and our world together took on a new luster. We were married on January 15, 1965. Doctor Schweitzer would have turned 90 on the day before our wedding. More than 50 years have flown by and I am writing about him in a book about *'ultimate caregiving.'* Amazing how life works.

The reason I write about Albert is because he really got it. He acted in unselfish love for the good of others. He once said:

> *"... for years I have been giving myself out in words, but this new form of activity would not be merely talking about the religion of love, but actually putting it into practice."*
>
> Albert Schweitzer

That was *'unselfish love in action.'* Thank you doctor.

A Personal Character Lesson.

It was 2 am. My head was spinning and I felt desperate. I looked at 12 year-old Jessica sleeping peacefully in front of me. I could see her eyes moving under her closed eye-lids. She was dreaming. I couldn't help but wonder...*'what was she dreaming?'*

I looked back at the papers before me. Our vaccine injury claim had been rejected by Health & Human Services lawyers. It did not make sense. Something was wrong. I was so tired, I wanted to quit... I looked back at Jessica, looking like an angel. Nope.

More Than a Cartoon

I was not giving up. I could not give up. I was committed. I loved her and somehow I would endure and come out on top.

I said a quick prayer, shook my head, took a drink of strong coffee. I started over again for the umpteenth time. Suddenly I noticed something... there it was... the answer. I saw the key mistake.

Adversity makes us stronger. I believe that, because I have experienced it. People are always saying... 'what does not kill you...makes you stronger!' Actually a lot of truth in that.

As caregivers, it is a principle from which we should take heart. We can grow stronger. We can grow into a better person. We can overcome our circumstances, and as we do, the scales fall off of our eyes and we begin to see the privilege of helping the helpless.

> *"The result of the voyage*
> *does not depend on the speed*
> *of the ship, but on whether*
> *or not it keeps a true course."*
>
> Albert Schweitzer

As we learn to survive, our overall confidence is slowly growing.

The torment and the revelation I was experiencing in the middle of that warm summer night, as I sat watching Jessica's sweet little dreams, was just one of many breakthroughs.

But I never forgot the lesson. Commitment and unselfish love grew stronger in my heart and gave me the strength to endure with an increased *confidence*. It kept me on a truer course.

Lessons from JESSICA

Growing CONFIDENCE.

Arnold Gold Photo   1984

Trust in Your Future.

Lessons from JESSICA

Chapter 9

Growing Confidence.

Trust in Your Future.

Viktor, Agnes and Albert, were not born with *'overcoming the world confidence'* but the evidence shows that they all had it.

In the caregiving world, I think we could agree that it is another facet we need to develop. I don't think we can just choose to be confident and acquire it immediately. That does not work.

There are some things that we can actively choose that will give us motivation and better morale, but some qualities we have to exercise to develop. We have to do some heavy lifting to become stronger. We can learn from others, we can learn from doing and we can learn from failing. Confidence is a big part of faith.

Suppose you want to learn to fly. Unless you are a bird or have super powers, you have a challenge. For centuries mankind dreamed of flying. This led to all kinds of experiments, many of them with disastrous results, but eventually we flew all the way to the moon and back. That kind of confidence took time.

Today if I want to fly, all I have to do is buy a ticket and... zoom!

As *'caregivers'* we are more like private pilots. We need a vehicle that can harness existing and universal principles to overcome the challenges necessary, get off the ground, and stay airborne. We need the confidence to do all of that... including landing safely.

Lessons from JESSICA

Trust and Confidence.

I was looking down at Jessica as she lay in her hospital bed in the Children's Intensive Care Unit. She was all wrapped and taped up, with tubes coming out. She looked like a medical experiment gone wrong. Yikes. I felt her warm little grip as our eyes met.

I was thinking about a dream that Jessica's cousin Kacey had a few months before we had decided, or even thought about scheduling, Jessica's scoliosis operation. In her remarkable dream Kacey had spoken with Jessica who walked up to her, and said among other things, "..tell my mom and dad I love them and *I will* be okay..."

We had puzzled over that amazing dream. Now the '*I will*' part stood out clearly in my mind. It was an assurance that we needed.

Jessica was only supposed to be in the hospital for three or four days and then home. We were now in our third week and stalled.

Sources of Confidence.

Sometimes confidence comes from unusual places, but more often than not, it comes from a steady progression of learning to cope and staying the course. Sometimes we need to hear from other caregivers. Sometimes we need to learn to trust others with our precious one. That learned confidence breeds hope.

Others with confidence help our confidence. Our experiences help us and may help others, as we humbly share our victories and trials. Remember Albert, who demonstrated with his life of service that '*delay is not defeat.*' With that perspective, there is no '*defeat*' in '*ultimate caregiving.*' Just bumps in the road.

Faith, Confidence & Hope.

Faith is the confident assurance of things not seen. *Confidence* in the things that are worthy breeds hope. *Hope* helps us find and keep the right *perspective*.

The good news is that all of these, combined with *commitment, endurance* and *unselfish love,* are inspirational and contagious. Doctor Schweitzer's radical decision and shocking life-changes inspired Helene Bresslau, who later became his wife.

Together they inspired their small circle of remaining friends who supported them, and eventually, that resulted in the unleashing of their healing medical mission. Forty years later the world acknowledged Albert & Helene's unselfish humanitarian efforts.

Through the activation of our faith, confidence and hope, we can trust the future. Unselfish love expressed in our actions never fails.

As caregivers we do not labor in vain. I believe we are privileged to walk that path. I think history shows that it is a path that leads to blessings. The path less traveled, the path of the caregiver.

Lessons from JESSICA

The Miracle of HOPE.

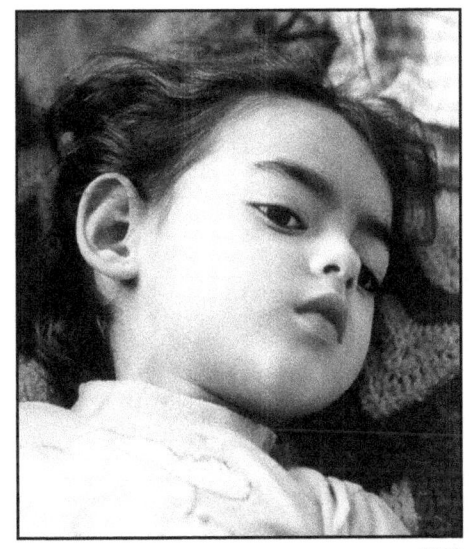

1982

Confidence Breeds Hope.

Lessons from JESSICA

Chapter 10

The Miracle of Hope.

Confidence Breeds Hope

Viktor Frankel had every reason to be hopeless.

His circumstances were horrific. He and his loved ones were separated. His first child was forcibly aborted. All around he saw death and deprivation. Hopelessness permeated the frigid air.

In the mire of the concentration camp many had no hope. The easy way out was to run to the electric fence surrounding his prison and grab the high voltage wire and escape through death.

While laying railroad tracks in sub zero temperatures he made a great discovery which changed his life forever. He later shared it around the world and countless others took hope from his insight into the essence of life and the salvation of man through love.

Viktor began to think of his young wife and his love for her. He realized that in spite of their physical separation, despite the agony of his cirumstances, she could be present within him.

> "...I understood how a man who has nothing left
> in this world still may know bliss, be it only for
> a brief moment, in the contemplation of his beloved."
>
> Viktor Frankel

He could clearly see, that those who had *hope*, who held on to a *vision* of the future, were most likely to survive their ordeal.

Lessons from JESSICA

Hope is a Vision of the Future.

By definition *'hopelessness'* is the despair you feel when you have abandoned all hope of comfort or success. Viktor saw that all around him everyday, but through his love within, his hope was growing and he survived and others survived through his confident hope in the future.

At the end he was very ill. Avoiding sleep for fear he would not wake up, he created a book, first in his mind and later writing it down on stolen scraps of paper. He was declaring in this small feat, his confident vision for the future. He was focused on helping others through his observations and insights into man's search for meaning. It became his life's work.

He was only delayed. He was not defeated. He held on to his vision of the future. And his very real hope was realized..

Hope and *'Ultimate'* Caregiving.

I often watch Jessica as she is sleeping. It is a bittersweet time. As she lays there sleeping like an angel with her soft delicate hands cradling her head, she looks perfectly normal.

Sometimes she will dream and I watch her eyes moving under her closed eyelids. It is especially sweet when she smiles and moves her legs as if she is walking somewhere. She is somewhere where there is no affliction, and she can run across meadows and run her hands through the fragrant wildflowers and laugh with joy.

In my minds eye as one of her caregivers... I can share that joy.

The Miracle of Hope.

Hope is complicated. It is something that you can not really seek and find. It seems to me from my experiences, and the much more dramatic experiences of others, that hope is a by-product of aligning ourselves with the principles I am sharing with you.

Choices we Control.

Commitment	*...get on board.*
Endurance	*...hang on tight.*
Unselfish Love	*...feel the power.*
Friendship	*...reach out for help.*
Perspective	*...choose wisely.*

Long Term Benefits of our Choices.

Character	*...stay on the path.*
Confidence	*...learn to take off.*
Hope	*...have a vision for the future.*

Hope does not depend on our circumstances. Hope does not depend on our past. Hope does not depend on our wealth.

I join with Viktor, Agnes, and Albert in declaring that hope is possible in any circumstance. Hope wells up in our mind and soul no matter where we are or what happens to us. We can have hope.

Hope is a miracle of the human soul. If we drill down deeply, hope will spring up in our hearts. And once it does it never stops.

We can be beaten down and endure to the end with the miracle of hope. If we put our faith in things that are worthy of our trust and stay patient, miracles can happen.

Lessons from JESSICA

Where is My PATIENCE?

Arnold Gold Photo　　　　　　1984

Running Out of it?

Lessons from JESSICA

Chapter 11

Where is My Patience?

Running Out of It?

"Oh, Lord give me patience... and give it to me... NOW!"

Wow. Funny but true. Been there... done that... many times.

To be *patient* means to endure trying circumstances with an even temper. It can also describe a person who requires medical care.

So *patience* is a state of endurance under difficult circumstances, which, looking even deeper, is persevering in the face of delay or provocation without acting on that annoyance or becoming angry as a result. So you could say to yourself, *'I need to be patient with my patient.'* Shakespeare phrased it, *"Patience in adversity."* My generation would say, *"Stay cool."* or *"Chill out, dude!"* as my kids would put it. My experience tells me, *'Easier said than done.'*

No question about it, *patience* is a very big part of caregiving.

Patience Thy Name is Caregiver.

Anne was born April 14, 1866 in a small town in Massachusetts. She grew up in poverty and at the age of five contracted an eye disease which severely compromised her sight. Her mother died when she was only eight years old. She was eventually sent to a poor house for children with her brother Jimmie. Soon he died leaving her all alone. Although physically sight challenged, she

Lessons from JESSICA

had a remarkable vision for her future within her heart. Hearing about schools for the blind, she became determined to get an education and escape from her abject poverty. When a special commission came to visit her children's home for the poor, she tagged around behind them, looking for her chance to speak up.

Eventually she found the chance and courageously asked them for help. It worked. Soon they sent her to a special school for the blind. Anne was on the path to a more purpose filled life.

She had never been to school and was humiliated by her ignorance and lack of social graces. She often lost her patience and her temper, which got her in trouble. But she was tremendously motivated and very bright and soon was learning and advancing rapidly. She was delayed but not defeated.

Anne Sullivan graduated as valedictorian of her class in 1886. At her graduation speech, from the *Perkins School for the Blind*, she made this visionary comment,

> *"...duty bids us go forth into active life.*
> *Let us go cheerfully, hopefully and earnestly, and set*
> *ourselves to find our especial part.*
>
> *When we have found it, willingly and faithfully perform it;*
> *for every obstacle we overcome, every success*
> *we achieve, tends to bring man closer to God."*
>
> Anne Sullivan

Down in Tuscumbia, Alabama, little Helen was waiting to fulfill Anne Sullivan's sweet vision. Soon they would meet.

Running Out of It?

Helen Adams Keller.

The very year that Ann left the squalor of the Tewksbury Almshouse and entered her first formal schooling at the Perkins School, little Helen was born. She was a bright and precocious child. She began to speak at six months and was walking when she was one. And then disaster pounced.

In 1882 she developed a very high fever. Although it lasted only a few days it left her sightless and unable to hear. She was only 18 months old. As she grew, she struggled with her affliction.

In 1887 the Keller family wrote to the Director of the Perkins School, looking for a governess for Helen who was deaf, blind and mute. Caring for Helen was becoming increasingly difficult.

He recommended the newly graduated, Anne Sullivan.

Helen by this time was a rather stubborn and spoiled student. Anne was only 21 but was a very mature, motivated and gifted teacher. She was about to meet her 'especial part.' Helen's world was about to change. Anne's world was about to change.

Their world was changing forever when, 'willing and faithful' Anne, met 'her obstacle to overcome,' Helen. Sparks were about to fly and what happened next, some would even call 'a miracle.'

Helen would later write:

> "...I felt approaching footsteps. I reached out my hand as I supposed to my mother. Some one took it, and I was caught up and held close in the arms of her who

Lessons from JESSICA

> *had come to reveal all things to me,
> and, more than all things else, to love me..."*
>
> Helen Keller

Helen graduated from college, *cum laude* in 1904, at age 24.

Patience for Miracle Workers.

What is interesting about Anne, the unlikely caregiver, and Helen the improbable care receiver, is the two perspectives we can see.

Helen was locked in a physical prison, with no escape in sight. She was helpless to improve her position. Along comes Anne who was at best a long shot to become a 'miracle worker.' Anne unlocks Helen's prison and frees her mind to soar. Helen becomes a force in the world, an inspirational speaker, an author and eventually her life story becomes an *'academy award winning'* motion picture.

It is possible that Helen, if her parents had followed the mainstream advice, they were getting, could have died in obscurity. But because of her committed, loving caregiver she was released and began to share her story as a care receiver and millions are hearing her story. Through caregiving her *soul* was emancipated.

How many lives were enriched and blessed and given hope, by this caregiving success story?

The 'miracle' was in the commitment and unselfish love that endured for a lifetime. I happen to believe that unselfish love never fails. Ultimately when we stay on the path we are never defeated, maybe delayed, but never defeated. That keeps me patient. The remarkable story of Anne and Helen should give us as caregivers, a renewed sense of perspective. The blessing of touching a soul.

Behind the Veil.

There are some of us as caregivers, who may never see the release from and overcoming of affliction, to the degree that Anne and Helen experienced it.

Renée and I have experienced a few glimmers of hope. We have had some experiences that we treasure, moments that have confirmed to us that Jessica is in there and knows us, and appreciates our love and care for her.

We keep our perspective with Jessica. One day at a time. We have great hope and confidence in our ultimate future together

Unselfish love is always patient. Self-love is impatient.

When I consider the times that I *'lose my patience,'* it is usually because I have my own self-interest at heart. Things are not going MY way. I am being inconvenienced. My focus is on myself.

I believe sometimes we confuse self gratification with patience.

"Lord I would be more patient if you would just let me have my own way." And I am thinking, ' *I better get my own way or there will be big trouble!'*

Here is what works. Think of the helpless person you are caring for. If you can, go to them and watch them sleeping quietly. Think how you would feel if that was you. How much would you appreciate loving help with your affliction? Got the picture?

We may never pass this way again. Love them and be *patient*.

Lessons from JESSICA

The Fruit of BLESSINGS.

Arnold Gold Photo   1984

Flowing from Sacrifice.

Lessons from JESSICA

Chapter 12

The Fruit of Blessings.

Flowing from Sacrifice.

Many of my ancestors were farmers. For generations they tilled the rich, flat clay plains of Illinois. Some of them still do.

My father grew up on a farm with his brothers and a sister. He often would say quite wryly that, *"...farmers are the biggest gamblers in the world. Every year they bet their farm on something they have absolutely no control over... the weather!"*

But they keep at it. I think most farmers are optimists.

I have trouble growing grass in my yard. Thank goodness for sod.

I guess I am missing the *'good farmer'* gene. My crops fail.

I have always been impressed with the farmer's sense of perspective. I like the way they plant trees and orchards and then wait years, sometimes generations, for the fruits of their labors. They live one day at a time, with one eye on the weather forecast and the other on the horizon. They also have great vision.

They plant an apple tree and carefully care for it until it bears fruit. How sweet that first apple must taste, a reward for their efforts.

Caregiving is like that. It can take a lifetime, but if done right, it produces wonderful fruit in our lives. The fruit of blessings.

Lessons from JESSICA

Blessings Flow from Sacrifice.

Based on our experience as caregivers for most of our lives, and the study of other caregivers, I really believe that sacrifice and unselfish love lead to rich blessings. I had to laugh when I read this comment from sweet little Agnes,

> "...I know that God will not give me anything I can't handle. I just wish he didn't trust me so much."
>
> Mother Teresa

I remember clearly the first day at the doctor's office that I heard Jessica's little heart beat and we realized rather unexpectedly... we were expecting! I loved her fiercely from that moment on.

The doctor gave us the option to destroy her. To stop that innocent little heart was unthinkable. That would have been the real tragedy. Not what unexpectedly came later.

Even now after many years of tests and surgeries and blood samples and 24 hour care, I would not change my decision to love and keep her close. Jessica *'the blessed one'* has truly been a blessing in our lives. She is still a blessing every day, and I believe she has taught us so much, about so many wonderful things.

The most amazing thing that has dawned on me after so many years, is what a privilege it is to be a caregiver. To help the helpless is to mirror God's efforts on our behalf. A wise choice.

With great sacrifices come great blessings.

> "The best and most beautiful things in the world cannot be seen or touched. They must be felt with the heart."
>
> Helen Keller

Flowing from Sacrifice

The Price.

Let's look at this as honestly as possible.

Most of us do not run around looking to sacrifice ourselves. Remember our definition of genuine love is unselfish love. With unselfish love *'sacrifice'* is both possible and more likely. Easy to see that demonstrated in the lives of Viktor, Agnes, Albert, Helen and Anne. They are the poster children of self-sacrifice.

But you and I are not. We may aspire to that. We may easily see their shining example and be comforted in our own personal journey. That is why I share their stories. They got it. They found the right path and they reaped the blessings of their journeys.

Each one of them experienced *'life'* differently, but rose to victory through the very same principles I am sharing with you. I have tested and tried them. They resonate with my own personal experiences. Just like the principles of flight will work for anyone regardless of the size of the aircraft, the principles of *'ultimate caregiving'* will work for anyone.

However, by it's very nature caregiving requires sacrifice.

You will give up something valuable. Your freedom, your lifestyle, your friends or relatives, your treasure, but you do not have to live in sorrow and gloom. In fact, as a caregiver who sees the benefit in the path ahead, you gain great blessings through your sacrifice.

You can turn sorrow into *joy.*

Lessons from JESSICA

Amazing JOY.

2012

Adding Everything Up.

Lessons from JESSICA

Chapter 13

Amazing Joy.

Adding Everything Up.

My wife Renée, was deserted by her mother as a small child. She was raised by her father, who was 44 years old when she was born. She had a very strained relationship with her mother and was deeply hurt by her childhood experiences. And yet in my mind, when I think of the word *joy*, I see her smiling face. She is the light that shines with joy. And yet, on the other hand, I have heard her sobs and seen her tears. I know how deeply her heart is broken.

How is that possible? Where does such joy come from?

Seeking Joy.

Before we were married, Renée and I were very like-minded about one thing. We wanted a stable and a happy home. We wanted answers to life's deeper questions. Neither one of us grew up in a Christian home and we wanted something better for our family. We were drawn to investigate the Bible and its promises. We were both pretty much in the dark at that point. We were seeking more.

So before we were married, we began to explore the subject. After we were married, we decided to read the Bible from cover to cover. And we did. We found the answers we were looking for.

I don't know why you are reading this book or what you believe, but it would be dishonest of me to not completely share all of my heart with you. I believe, if you honestly and openly investigate, you will agree with me that God is the *ultimate caregiver*. In the *Appendix* you will find some resources to help you on your way.

Amazing Joy.

The reason I am sharing my personal faith and life foundation with you, is because of the topic... JOY. After much study and after over 50 years as a Christian and also spending most of my life as a 24/7 caregiver, I have to conclude that there is something supernatural about joy. The paradox is that you can have joy and a broken heart at the same time. It can tip the scales in our lives. Joy is a fruit that we can experience that comes straight from heaven.

If God exists and loves us and gave us written instructions on how to be happy and joyful in our lives, then that would be the most important book ever written. That would be the Bible.

As parents, we are caregivers to our children. As a *'caregiver'* we are responsible to help and care for someone who may be helpless. In both cases, there are certain tasks we must do and routines we must execute on a daily basis. There are principles that must be followed. Medications, all kinds therapy, feedings, changing diapers and so on. The structure is needed for their well being.

We do these routine disciplined tasks on an ongoing basis, day in and day out. We do not do it for the reward. We do it for the love of that person and respect for the dignity and worth of their soul. We are there, willing to help. That is our motivation and purpose.

So, even though there are boundaries and structure and principles to follow, the reason we do it is mainly *relational*. We love them

Lessons from JESSICA

and so we act on that love to help the helpless. God does the very same thing for us. He has given us principles and structure but he is doing that, because of love. Because God is love, He helps us in our own helplessness to have joy. He seeks to *protect* and *provide*.

There are hundreds of verses in the Bible about joy and rejoicing and being joyful. Here is one that speaks to my soul:

> *"I have told you these things so that you will be filled with my joy. Yes, your joy will overflow. This is my commandment: Love each other in the same way I have loved you. There is no greater love than to lay down one's life for one's friends."*
>
> Jesus Christ in John 15:11-13(NLT)

Rejoice! We can all have joy. And we need to enjoy it when we do.

The Power of Joy.

Entire books are being written on the topic of joy. Why?

Joy appears to be a nebulous and vaporous thing. It can be everywhere and nowhere. It can be very tangible and then vanish in an instant. Our little friend Agnes, noticed that people surrounded by wealth and luxury may not have it. On the other hand, Viktor observed, that people who were prisoners in a cruel and frigid concentration camp, obviously had joy in abundance.

Old Albert was aware of people who were sitting around, talking about and contemplating joy, but did not have it themselves, and noticed other very busy people, who were not seeking joy but were actively serving and caring for others, who found it in their hearts.

Adding Everything Up

Helen was able to feel joy in her heart in spite of her severe disabilities. She was able to pass that joy out of the darkness to us, helping to light our world. She was rejoicing in her affliction.

Joy is truly amazing. A great thing. I think it is a God-sized thing.

Defining Joy.

Where does joy come from and where is it on the caregiving path? Let's look at what it isn't and then try to define it in our lives. First, let's narrow down the possibilities and look at what it is not.

What Joy is Not.

Joy is a critical facet of ultimate caregiving and it is often confused with many other things, which can lead to despair. Here is a list.

Joy is not... happiness. Joy is not... a choice. Joy is not... getting your own way. Joy is not... a lack of conflict. Joy is not... a life of ease. Joy is not... self contentment. Joy is not... our perspective. Joy is not... external. Joy is not... wealth. Joy is not... gloom.

One thing for sure, joy is not... natural. More supernatural.

Night & Day.

Joy is like light. It can shine brightly or be hidden. It can be blinding and then snuffed out, and then reappear without warning to fill our hearts to overflowing.

I can imagine a summer storm with dark billowing clouds and lightning and thunder, and rain beating down, and then it is over

Lessons from JESSICA

and suddenly the sun breaks through and seems brighter than ever, instantly blinding and refreshing everything it touches. Such an exhilarating experience, seeing the beams of light come through and chase the gloom away and breathing deeply the fresh sweet air.

Joy and light just go together. That is what real amazing joy is like.

Joy for Living.

What is the absence of joy? Gloom, darkness & depression. That is the polar opposite of joy.

Try this. Go get a light bulb and hold it in your hand. Then with the power of your mind and body try to make it light up.

It cannot be done without connecting the bulb to the power source that it needs. Our *soul* is like that bulb. It is made to shine and will shine brightly, if we connect to the power source. You can even cover that lighted bulb under a bushel basket, but when lighted it will still be shining brightly.

We can make that choice. We can choose the right path.

We cannot *make* ourselves full of joy on our own efforts, but we can *choose* to seek the power source. A critical choice for joy.

Joy in Caregiving.

If we have faith in the *'ultimate caregiver'* and embrace the unique value of every human soul, we will become an ultimate caregiver. Our hearts will be full of joy even though they may be broken. We will come out of the gloom and depression and into the marvelous and comforting light of joy. We will bear the fruit of JOY.

It has been my experience that if we make a commitment, endure to the end, embrace unselfish love, find the right perspective, strengthen our character, grow in confidence, have hope for the future and be patient, we will find the blessing and joy in the privilege of caregiving.

That is the path to *ultimate* caregiving.

Considering *FAITH*

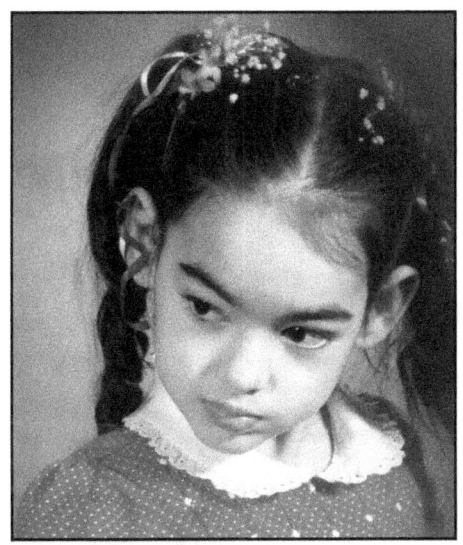

Growing Up with Jessica   2005

Someone is at The Door.

Lessons from JESSICA

Chapter 14

Considering Faith.

Someone is at the Door.

As I sat in the crowded gym watching a Billy Graham film, I felt something stirring in my heart. A warm pressure was growing. The story on the screen was *The Restless Ones*, a story of a teen in conflict, not really a bad kid, just a kid looking for answers.

In my mind's eye, I flew back to an event that happened to me as a teen. It had been the first time that I had ever considered eternity, as I looked down the barrel of a loaded gun. I was pinned against a chain link fence on a dusty, remote path, in Reno, Nevada.

It was my first week in town after moving from Boise. I had unwittingly trespassed on a local gangs '*turf*' and now I was in trouble. It was hot. I was trapped and outnumbered about 10 to 1. I glanced around. There was no one apt to come to my rescue.

I remember thinking, '*...to escape I would have to free myself from the gang members holding me, cover three or four feet and wrestle the gun away... on the other hand all the gang leader would have to do was twitch one finger...*' I considered what would happen then. All I saw was darkness... nothing. I was shocked to consider that. I was facing possible death, and I was a 14 year old kid and unprepared.

I turned back to the film, but I could not ignore the yearning in my heart. My heart was thumping. It felt like someone was knocking.

Lessons from JESSICA

Josh McDowell, Skeptic.

At about the same time that I was considering eternity, a young man half a world away was facing his own crisis of faith. A nineteen year old Josh McDowell stood transfixed in Glasgow, Scotland as he stared at the fragments of a 1600 year old *New Testament* manuscript.

Here is how he described his experience:

> *"As I stood there, a strange and unexpected feeling washed over me. Though I could not read or understand a single line of the Greek in which that manuscript was written, those words seemed to reach out to me in an almost mystical way. Even though I was an unbeliever at the time, I sensed an uncanny power about those words."*
>
> Josh McDowell

Josh McDowell had left Michigan and traveled to **Glasgow University** to do research to disprove Christianity. His goal was to specifically show that the Bible was historically unreliable and that Jesus was by *'no means the son of God.'* He was to spend months researching in the finest libraries in Europe, devouring dozens of books and speaking with many leading scholars. He finally concluded:

> *"Leaning back in my chair, I stared up at the ceiling and spoke these words aloud '...It's true!'"*
>
> Josh McDowell

Josh embraced the truth of that moment, and he chose to become a believer in Christianity, even as the emotions of what that truly meant, washed over him. Today he is considered one of the world's leading defenders and teachers of Christianity. That is *real* faith.

Years later we would meet in Boise, Idaho, as I stood nervously clutching my first manuscript of *'Growing Up with Jessica.'*

Making a Choice.

The film had ended, and as I sat there I knew I wanted the peace in my heart that was missing. Over the last year Renée and I had been reading a chapter in the Bible every night. I agree with Josh, it is no ordinary book. I have read hundreds, even thousands of books, but nothing ever affected my heart in that way.

I stayed and talked to another young man there at the meeting. He pointed to the Bible verse on the large overhead banner.

> *"For God so loved the world that he gave his only son, so that whoever believes in him should not perish, but have everlasting life."*
>
> John 3:16 (NLT)

Honestly, I did not know for sure if that was true, but with all my thumping heart, I sincerely wanted it to be true. And that is exactly what I told him when he asked me if I believed.

He prayed for me and my heart exploded with an indescribable joy. It was a feeling I had never known. Emotions washed over me. I felt a swelling in my heart that dramatically confirmed my prayer.

I was 20 years old and my journey of faith had just begun. How thankful I would be over and over again as the years went flying by. Our children and grandchildren have been born and are growing up in the faith that I found that day. I feel completely blessed.

Lessons from JESSICA

Josh was to become so very important along the way, as my skeptical faith grew stronger over the years. The first book by Josh I remember, is called '*Evidence that Demands a Verdict*'. It is a book that began when a 19 year old skeptic with an honest an open mind, encountered a loving and gracious God.

Through that encounter, I believe, Josh has grown to become one of the greatest living advocates for Christianity, alive today. If you want to consider the truth he has discovered and documented, you will find a partial listing of his books in the *Appendix*.

Faith & Caregiving.

I am not a preacher or evangelist or a great Bible scholar. I am just someone who wants to help caregivers survive and thrive.

I am an honest man who is sharing the truth of my life. It would be dishonest to not acknowledge the importance of faith in my life and my family's life. I have never written some of these things down before and I may even share a few other experiences, that only my family knows, but I must tell you the whole story.

The Christian faith we discovered so many years ago has kept us going over the years. The decision that I made that night over 50 years ago has been all important in our ability to survive and thrive. It has allowed us to learn our '*lessons*' from Jessica.

The path to ultimate caregiving leads through the valley of faith. I also honestly believe that the '*object*' of our faith must be worthy.

We can only do so much on our own strength. We grow old. We grow weak. We are surrounded by daily fears and questions. It is such a blessing to know that eternal comforts are available.

> *"Come to me, all of you who are weary and carry heavy burdens, and I will give you rest."*
>
> Jesus Christ in Matthew 11:28 (NLT)

I am saying to you in all sincerity that as a Christian since 1965 and a 24/7 caregiver since 1978, that these deeper things of life are true and we are now experiencing God's *'ultimate caregiving.'*

Choose Wisely.

I would be the last person to force anything upon you. You and I must make our own decisions. I just acknowledge the fact that we must choose wisely. I remember to this day the chill that I felt as I looked into that gun barrel and considered the darkness.

All I can offer you is my testimony. God is real and places our protection and comfort uppermost. I have studied and learned for a lifetime, and I must conclude as Josh did that day long ago after concluding his studies, *"...It's true... It's true... It's true!"*

Answers are Available.

Perhaps you don't believe. Maybe you think Christianity is all a bunch of baloney. If you are intellectually honest and are not afraid of the answers you may find, then please take the time to check things out. In the *Appendix* you will find a small list of helpful books. A place to start. It is my fervent prayer that you will find what you need.

Lessons from JESSICA

Help for the HELPLESS.

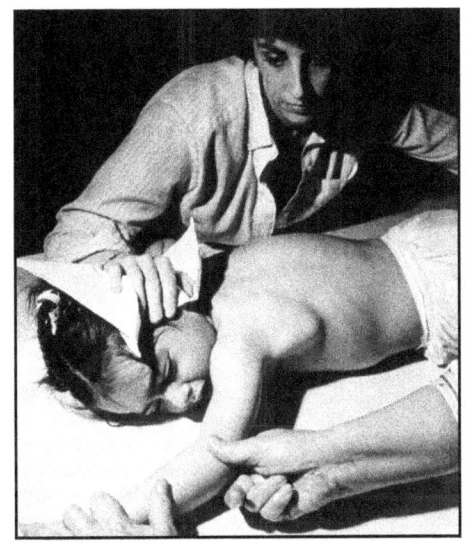

Arnold Gold Photo   1984

Who is the Helpless One?

Lessons from JESSICA

Chapter 15

Help for the Helpless.

Who is the Helpless One?

I tried to look into Renée eyes... but everything was blurry. I could sense the concern in her voice. Her hands were trembling.

I cleared my throat, and as I panted for breath, raspingly said,

"I think I can get up... and make it out to the car...one time..." I gasped,*"...but that is it...I need to get to the emergency room."*

Even in my blurry state I could see her shock and disbelief.

Have you ever been completely or almost completely helpless?

If you have, you know the feeling. Someone else is responsible for you. You have lost your independence and free will. It is a trapped sensation that claws at your soul. It is hard not to panic when the alarm in your brain is clanging, *'...danger... danger!'*

I had been sick for about ten days. It started on a beautiful fall day as Renée and I walked on the Boise River Greenbelt. The sky was a brilliant blue made even more stark by all the color in the trees.

We walked and talked about my book **Growing Up with Jessica**. It was my first book & the culmination of over 25 years of caring for Jessica. It was due at the book publisher in about 10 days and I was wrapping it up. As I remember we were marveling at all of the

Lessons from JESSICA

many amazing things that had brought us to that point. Not to mention that Josh McDowell was writing the 'foreword.' Wow.

It was an amazing walk with the love of my life and came very close to being my last. I just did not feel at ease. *'Just tired,'* I thought to myself. Later that night we went to an Anne Murray concert. She is one of my favorite singers, but once again I felt restless and unable to settle down. I remember getting up and wandering around the auditorium. Nothing would put me at ease.

The next morning I was sick. For ten days I ran a low grade fever and made three trips to the doctor's office. Finally, on that fateful Sunday, I asked Renée to drive me to the hospital. I was helpless.

At Death's Door.

And so it came to be that on the very day that I had planned to submit my final files for my first book, I lay near death. I actually had one of those near death experiences. Not as dramatic as some I have heard of, but an amazing experience nonetheless.

I learned three things that day. Heaven is a real place, it is easy to die, and I was being comforted. My heart felt excited, like it would burst with joy. I remembered back to my first experience. I know that I have nothing to fear, but it was not my time to move on.

Maybe this sounds really crazy to you. I know it could, but I also know that it really happened. So there it is. No longer a secret. I take comfort in that experience and perhaps you can as well.

I was the care-receiver and I literally could not feed myself. A humbling experience for sure, but it was a very valuable time.

Who is the Helpless One?

Humbling Helplessness.

So after 25 plus years of being a *'caregiver,'* and feeding my youngest daughter Jessica with a spoon every day, I found myself being fed with a spoon as a *'care-receiver.'* An interesting transition. The whole experience, although difficult and traumatic for me and my family, was a very great learning opportunity for all of us. A humbling one, for me especially.

As the youngest in my family and the only male child, I tend to be rather independent minded. The fact that our family moved when I was in the first, fourth, seventh, ninth (twice) and tenth grade, also contributed to my own self sufficiency. I remember the last four times we relocated, when I was a teenager, my dad would just drop me off at the school and I would go inside and look for the office. It would go something like this:

"Hi... my name is Jimmy Walker... I just moved here and I need to sign up for school." I would say to the usually startled staff member, who would look anxiously around for my parents.

"Uhmm, okay... do you have a parent or guardian?"

"Yeah...why?"

Somehow I would always convince them that I was not from Mars, and if they would let me register, I would get the signature they needed from my dad. I would usually sign it later myself. I had learned how to forge my dad's signature on my report cards from about the seventh grade on. He was 'old school' and just expected to see the last report card of the year, the one that said I

Lessons from JESSICA

was moving on to the next grade. I was an *'underachiever.'*

As you can see I had a few character issues, but I had learned how to stand on my own two feet. In many situations I faced, I was all alone and had to work things out for myself. Like that one particular, hot and dusty day in Reno. All I had was myself.

There I was helpless, being spoon fed by my family members.

A Grateful Heart.

The whole hosptial experience was a jumble of emotions and highs and lows, but I emerged alive and a better person for it.

The most powerful emotion I now recall, was my complete surrender to gratitude. I was so grateful for the care given to me.

I don't know if you have had an experience like that. If you have you may know the feeling. Surrounded by all of those people, all dedicated to helping you survive and thrive was almost indescribable. Nurses, doctors, all kinds of therapists, and most of all my family. My family never left me alone. They were always there. Especially my son Jon and daughter Jamie.

They took turns caring for me and helping Renée care for Jessica. I felt so humbled and grateful. I think Renée, Jon & Jamie were the critical factor in my survival... a point driven home during my *'exit interview'* at the hospital.

I noticed that the nurse conducting my exit interview and giving me instructions, was the head of the *'Respiratory Therapy Department.'* I asked her if that was normal. Here is her reply:

"No. I do not normally do this. I wanted to meet you. I am very curious how you survived your 'silent' pneumonia."

"How I survived what? I don't get it!"

"Mr. Walker you had a very lethal form of respiratory infection... we call it the 'silent death' around here. 99 out of 100 patients who contract it do not walk out of the hospital."

"Whoa.." I said as I tried to digest that.

"I am curious how you did it."

In my mind I saw a whirl of things, a roller coaster of emotions, "My family... I finally said. "...their love and caregiving, was the difference...Yes... no doubt they were the critical difference!"

The Caregiving Equation.

As caregivers we need to keep our focus on the 'care-receiver.' That may sound obvious, but it is easy to see our caregiving as a chore to be done and the care receiver as an 'object' rather than a person.

We get in a routine and we forget that we are dealing with a thinking, breathing, body, mind and soul. That person may not respond or be able to express their gratitude, but our attitude is important. We are transmitting a signal. Do we feel privileged or somehow enslaved?

I remember when I was very close to death and helpless and suffering in silence, my sense of the cares and attitudes of those around me was heightened. It was as if I could see into their heart and soul. There was one technician in quite close proximity to me, and as I watched her I sensed great pain in her heart.

I can not explain it, but it was so real, that I reached out and took her hand and croaked, *"It's okay, everything will be okay."* She was of course startled. No, I was not on drugs. I later heard her say that her son had been arrested the night before. Somehow I could sense her anguish. It was loud and clear.

I am not some mystic or holy man, nor do I want to be, but that experience made me think that since I am no different than anyone else, perhaps it was my *'helplessness'* that raised my sensitivity. Perhaps when we are physically trapped in our helplessness we are more sensitive in our mind and soul.

Helping the Helpless.

I have shared some very personal things with you that I hope you will accept in the same spirit I am giving them to you. To be an ultimate caregiver we need to put ourselves in the place of the care receiver. We need to see caregiving as a great privilege.

Perhaps we need to become more sensitive. Just imagine that the person you may be a caregiver for, could read your mind as you care for them. What would that do to your perspective?

I have shared my faith with you. So I hope you can understand my perspective. I think God can see our helplessness as we help the helpless. God wants to be our ultimate caregiver and comforter.

Ask yourself this, *'what is one human soul worth?'*

Consider the SOUL.

2012

What is a Soul Worth?

Lessons from JESSICA

Chapter 16

Consider the Soul.

What is a Soul Worth?

I believe that as caregivers or care receivers, we all have a *'body,'* a *'mind'* and a *'soul.'* Each entity is a part of who we are. Each one exerting a certain amount of control and influence over our actions. These things all add up to our life and its meaning.

Everyday we write our own unique personal story which becomes part of our memory and the memories of others in our circle of influence. What has become increasingly clear to me after 70 plus years, is that, *'our life is in our memories.'*

Body, mind and soul. Each one has its own unique characteristics.

The Dwelling Place.

Our *physical body* is where our mind and soul is residing as we live our daily lives. Our body has it's very definite sights, smells and sounds, as well as the basic input from our five senses.

Sight, hearing, touch, smell and taste are commonly accepted. They allow our physical body to function, survive and learn. They are the reason selfishness or self-love comes so easily to us.

Our physical bodies are programmed to protect us from life's dangers, survive and hopefully learn from our mistakes.

Lessons from JESSICA

The Wheelhouse.

Our *mind* is where our thoughts live. An interesting and undeniable fact is that we can only actively have *one* thought at a time. Just one thought at a time.

We may be able to think a chain of thoughts very quickly, but our conscious thoughts, you know that little voice in our head, is stuck in *'serial mode,'* as my computer geek friends would put it.

This serial attribute of our mind is a real asset as we learn to make choices. Linking one good choice to another for instance, can change our course for the better, and fortify our character development. Think how hard it would be to make a decision if our mind was flooded with many thoughts at the same instant.

That kind of babble, would inevitably lead to *'analysis paralysis.'*

So we have constant sensory input, controlled and regulated and influenced by our minds, all generally focused on number one. Naturally, that would be, our own self interest and promotion.

Once again we come by self-love very easily. It is a natural outgrowth of our body and mind and our aspirations to survive and pamper all of our in-born physical appetites. Some would call it the *'survival instinct.'*

Fortunately we also have something else with immeasurable value, that makes us whole and complete. Our immortal soul.

Unselfish love and real joy spring in abundance from the soul.

What is a Soul Worth?

The Essence.

Once again I am reminded, that entire books have been written on the *soul*. There are some who even dispute its existence.

As I have already shared, I did not start out as a Christian, but I can say, that after spending over 50 years as a Christian and over half of my life as a caregiver, I know that the human soul does exist. I also know that my daughter Jessica has one and it is worth as much as mine. Our souls do have immeasurable value.

I think it is important to emphasize, that every caregiver has a soul. Every care-receiver has one as well. The soul is the well of eternity.

Three Choices.

Will we be dominated by our body, mind or soul? We can choose. In life, it seems to me,, we have these three choices. We can be:

    ...*Body* Driven   ...*Mind* Driven   ...*Soul* Driven.

If we choose to let our body or mind, or both, dominate us, my experience concludes that we will end up seeking physical comfort, pleasure and security as we coddle ourselves and look out for good old number one. Let's be honest. We all have a natural tendency to do that.

Viktor Frankel.

Viktor Frankel noticed a stark contrast in his harsh prison camp environment. As he observed his fellow prisoners he saw two basic types of behavior.

Lessons from JESSICA

First, were those motivated by unselfish love, giving away their food to others. He called them *'saints.'* In stark contrast were the *'swine,'* who primarily sought to protect their own selfish, survival interests. They would collaborate with the enemy and cruelly betray their comrades. Pure *'selfishness'* in action.

The *'unselfish love'* he saw manifested in spite of the despair all around him, he described as, "*...the truth that Love is the ultimate and highest goal to which man can aspire...*" That would be, I believe, unselfish love in action. Soul driven love.

Mother Teresa.

Little Agnes, was sensitive to the prompting of her soul. She listened and acted with unselfish love and conviction over and over again, and became the beloved Mother Teresa we know.

She had discovered ultimate love. Soul driven love.

Josh McDowell.

Josh McDowell had a heart-breaking childhood and in his own words, "*...once had a lot of hatred, mainly toward my father, an alcoholic.*" As a teenager he tied his father up and attempted poisoning him. He grew up a hurt and angry young man.

He also grew up antagonistic towards Christianity and even traveled to Europe at the age of 19, with one goal, to disprove everything Christian.

He encountered God and was transformed. Now *soul driven*, his starving soul began devouring life's deep and eternal truths.

What is a Soul Worth?

Before his father died he was able to say, *"...Dad, I love you!"*

Josh is the author of over 140 books defending and sharing the faith he once sought to destroy. He is soul driven.

Albert Schweitzer.

Albert the gifted and talented musician, one day answered the calling of his soul to love and serve his fellowman. He put everything aside. He rejected the comfort and complacency his body and mind naturally desired. He chose to act on his love and compassion, as he endured criticism and the temptation to give up.

He tapped into his soul, and he stayed true to his calling and changed the lives of countless thousands. He was soul driven.

Anne Sullivan.

Refusing to sink into poverty and despair, she chose to discipline her mind and give herself over to her soul, and finding her...

> *"...especial part. When we have found it, willingly and faithfully perform it; for every obstacle we overcome, every success we achieve tends to bring man closer to God."*
>
> Anne Sullivan

Does that sound like someone who is driven by the comfort or pleasure of the mind and body? She followed the call of her soul.

Because Anne answered the urging of her soul, she became a *'miracle worker'* and we all have the unlikely blessings that flowed from the life of her care-receiver, Helen Keller.

Lessons from JESSICA

Helen Keller.

Little Helen found herself locked in her body, alone for the most part, with her mind and soul. She was in desperate need of care.

Because Anne was soul driven and answered the call, Helen was freed from her prison. She would later write of Anne:

> *"...When she came, everything about me breathed of love and joy and was full of meaning. She has never since let pass an opportunity to point out the beauty that is in everything, nor has she ceased trying in thought and action and example to make my life sweet and useful..."*
>
> Helen Keller

Helen would go on to emulate the sweet, soul driven unselfish love that Anne modeled so well. She herself became a *'miracle'* of inspiration, encouraging many others. Her soul burned brightly.

> *"The best and most beautiful things in the world cannot be seen or even touched. They must be felt with the heart."*
>
> Helen Keller

What is One Soul Worth?

As a longtime caregiver I have some insights into how things work where the *'...rubber meets the road.'* I believe we all have an immortal soul. I believe that the soul is the touchstone of the immortality spoken of in the Bible. I do not know if you do.

I also know that if you seek the answers to your questions and you

What is a Soul Worth?

are intellectually honest, you will find them. They are out there.

In the *Appendix* you will find some books and resources to help you if you want to know the truth about the *'deeper things of life.'*

One of the secrets of long term caregiving is to acknowledge the existence and infinite value of the soul. I repeat, I believe the soul is the well of eternity.

God is not up there somewhere or over there or over here. He is not found through dogmatic rules or theologians. What if God is in you already, waiting patiently to help you in your helplessness?

I believe He is not only in your soul, but is constantly knocking. Once we answer and open the door, we are on the path to being a *'soul driven'* person. Now that is a game changer.

> *"...And what do you benefit if you gain the whole world but lose your own soul? Is anything worth more than your soul?"*
>
> Jesus Christ in Mark 8:37 (NLT)

Choices We Control.

Commitment, Endurance, Unselfish Love, Friendship, Perspective, Faith, Helplessness, A Soul Driven life.

Long Term Benefits of our Choices.

Character, Confidence, Hope, Patience, Blessings, Joy, and one more ...*Understanding our Privilege.*

Lessons from JESSICA

It is Our PRIVILEGE.

Arnold Gold Photo   1984

The Greatest of Them All.

Lessons from JESSICA

Chapter 17

It is Our Privilege.

The Greatest of Them All.

The Beginning of Privilege.

What do you think of when you think of privilege? Silver spoons? Limos? Mansions and servants? An exclusive club membership?

The kind of privilege we are talking about here, is realizing what an honor it is to be a caregiver. You and I need to come to the full realization of the precious responsibility that we have, as the caregiver to another human soul, who is most likely helpless.

It helps if we can realize, that nothing is more valuable than a soul.

Can you think of any greater privilege that God could give you or I, than helping the helpless? God saw that we were helpless and out of love did something about it. We are blessed to be able to do the same for at least one person. That may be a big shift of gears.

The sooner that we embrace our role and understand the significance of our mission, the sooner we will see the joy in our *'ultimate caregiving.'* We should try to reach that perspective as soon as possible. The sooner the better. It is the right path.

Seeing and understanding our great privilege as a caregiver is the beginning of our ultimate victory, and peace of mind follows.

Lessons from JESSICA

Embracing Our Privilege.

The concepts and guidelines I have been sharing in this book are gleaned from our real life experiences. Someone said that *'hindsight is 20/20.'* It has been much easier to look back over the years and clearly see what worked, and what did not.

Experience is a great teacher. How much pain and frustration we would have been spared if someone had given us a clear path to follow. Even the *'professionals'* we have crossed paths with, didn't seem to have solid answers for us.

On one extreme you have the scientist, humanist driven crowd, who seems more interested in showing us how to rid ourselves, of what to them, seemed a burden.

> *"We can... you know eliminate this pregnancy..."*
>
> Family Practice Physician

Then after a few years, we began to hear lots of advice like this:

> *"You should put Jessica in an institution, so you can have a good life without 24/7 caregiving."*
>
> Healthcare Professional

Not really the *'soul driven'* advice we needed. In fact, in our case, we found much of the *'professional'* advice repulsive.

We were hearing a lot of that kind of *'body and mind'* driven advice as we struggled along. Of course, I do realize that there are situations where professional, clinical help may be necessary. In that case your caregiving role changes slightly. You will find

The Greatest of Them All.

yourself in a more supervisory and supportive role. However there are not enough places and beds available or the staff to care for the entire care-receiving population. According to some surveys I have read, just in the USA alone, there are over 60 million care givers.[1]

Most caregiving is at home and that trend will continue and even continue to grow in the future.

On the other extreme, we were receiving advice from our well meaning Christian friends. Here are some examples.

> " *Trust in the Lord, not your own understanding.*"
>
> Christian Pastor

> " *God has a plan for your lives.*"
>
> Christian friend

> " *We are praying for you and your family.*"
>
> Christian friend

Christian friends and pastors mean no harm and were sincere. The words they spoke are ultimately true, but because of their awkwardness and inexperience in the long term caregiving world, such platitudes ring hollow. Most don't know how to help.

Actions, even small ones done with great love, carry much more weight. We didn't need any more '*theory,*' we needed *application*. We needed an honest '*soul driven*' guide to follow.

As I have stated before, the premise of this book is to help and inspire those who are helping the helpless. The blessed caregivers, who love and care for the well being, of another soul.

Lessons from JESSICA

The Greatest of them All.

Unselfish love and faith are great motivators. They will take you a long way and overcome many heart breaks, but what we need as caregivers is a deep inspiration for the work we do.

I am not ever going to write a book about our failures... it would be too big! I do however, from time to time, pull back the curtain and share the blood and guts of our journey.

I can relate to little Agnes when she confirmed that "*...God would not give her anything He didn't think she could handle... she just wished he wouldn't trust her so much.*" So true it hurts.

It has only been in recent years that my eyes have been opened to see the full inspiration of caregiving. I realize now that we have been given a great privilege by God and the quicker we embrace that concept the quicker we acquire an immortal inspiration.

Everything makes sense then and starts to fall into place. We see the '*God perspective.*' We realize that we are partners with Jesus Christ as we go into action and help the helpless.

We are Helpless to Save Ourselves.

God comes to us, right to the door of our heart, and basically says, '*open the door and I will enter, and be your 'ultimate caregiver,' I will lighten your burdens, I will give you rest.*' God may not take our troubles away but he will care for us and help with the load. Our inspiration as caregivers should be like that. To love and care for a human soul and lighten their load. Blessed are the caregivers.

The Greatest of Them All.

A Glimpse of the Future.

I hope that you find this little book helpful. After writing *Growing Up with Jessica,* many people asked me if I would ever write another book about our experiences with her as we *'grew up.'*

My reply was always the same;

"I would, if I could see a way to help people who may be facing or going through, what we are experiencing."

"What would that book be about?"

"Well, I don't know for sure, but probably about the lessons we have learned, and how others could find their way quicker and easier. That would be great... a dream come true."

You are holding that dream in your hands. I hope and pray that it has helped you as a caregiver or caregiver supporter.

Help for the Helplessness.

At long last the scales fell off of our eyes and we realized we have been tasked with the greatest privilege of them all... *'caregiving.'*

> *"For three things I thank God every day of my life: Thanks that he has vouchsafed me knowledge of his works; that he has set in my darkness the lamp of faith; deep, deepest thanks that I have another life to look forward to... a life joyous with light and flowers and heavenly song."*
>
> Hellen Keller

The Undiscovered Land

Traveling in JessicaLand.

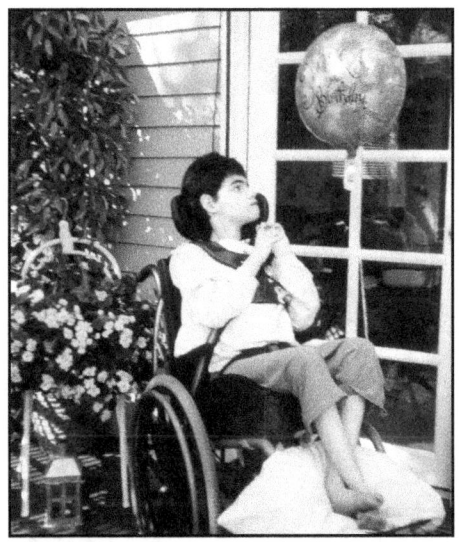

Jessica turns 21   1999

We 'Grew Up' with Jessica.

Lessons from JESSICA

Chapter 18

Traveling in JessicaLand.

We '*Grew Up*' with Jessica.

On August 25, 1978, a baby girl was born in Boise, Idaho. The next day we named her Jessica Elizabeth Walker.

We found out later that '*Jessica*' meant '*blessed one*' and '*Elizabeth*,' chosen because it was my mother's middle name, meant '*consecrated to God*.' At the time we thought that was all a very sweet bit of trivia. What an interesting combo.

'Blessed one... Consecrated to God...' wow... what a name, and what a sweet little girl. Based on the nurses observation of her long delicate fingers, '*...sure to be a concert pianist.*' I was thinking with a happy father's pride '*...absolutely!*' as visions of pianos danced in my head. It was the best of times for our family.

A few days later at work, I answered the phone, I could hear Renée sobbing and trying to talk. I sat bolt upright in my chair and spoke firmly into the phone,

"Hello Renée is that you? What is it... what's wrong?"

"It's J-Jessica, she moaned... *she can't come home with me!*"

"What!" What's happened?" My heart was on the floor, as I listened to her sobbing. That was the last thing I had expected.

Lessons from JESSICA

Finding Our Way.

When Renée and I entered the world of caregiving that hot August day so long ago, we were pretty confused. I think by and large that is where most of us are when unexpected things jump up in front of us. Suddenly our path is blocked. We take a detour that runs through hospitals, specialists, lab tests, all manner of x-rays, therapy sessions, nutritionists, and the list goes on.

What we wanted, was a simple *'normal'* life. What dawned on us slowly with Jessica, was the fact that this *was* our *'new normal.'*

We each struggled with that in different ways. You may now be where we were then. We floundered around for a long time. I was focused on our future needs, Renée was focused on changing the past, correcting everything and seeing Jessica normal again.

We failed and crashed and bloodied our noses running into walls.

The first few years we probably survived on our *stubbornness* as we tried to make sense of everything. We had our faith, and our love for our child of course, but we needed a path and the clear concise mental picture of how to stay on that path and go forward.

After many years, as I look back I see the sign posts along the path. I really do believe that the principles I am sharing in this book can help others get on the path quicker. If we had been presented this information back when we began, it would have been a blessing.

What I am sharing is based on our *'real'* experiences. It is my hope & prayer that you will be helped by these principles. And that as a caregiver may find your way to the blessings & joy that await you.

Priorities for Surviving & Thriving.

The first thing I wish we could have seen more clearly, were the three *'caregiving rails'* of Commitment, Endurance & Unselfish Love. These three need to be there first, and be solid as a rock, to keep you from crashing off the path. Here is a summary of all of the principles that I wish we had known when we began:

First: Commitment.

First, a *'Primary Caregiver'* needs to be totally committed to the recipient of their caregiving. If you are not totally committed sooner or later things will fall apart. It think it is true that *'unselfish love'* is in the DNA of commitment, but they *both* require a *choice* of your free will. That is why they have great value.

'Secondary Caregivers,' 'Friends' and *'Observers,'* must make a commitment to *support the caregivers* they know. A *'...small kindness done with great love,'* as Agnes would say, can make a huge difference. Who knows, it may be the critical difference. Every caregiver struggles, and they need your supportive love.

Second: Endurance.

The second rail that keeps you going straight and hanging on in the corners. It is linked to commitment. It is a fruit that only exists on the vine of commitment. Endurance keeps you loving and caring to the end, no matter what. It is how you get up when you are knocked down. To finish the course, you must finish.

> "A bend in the road is not the end of the road...
> Unless you fail to make the turn."
> Hellen Keller

Lessons from JESSICA

The big key to endurance, as I shared in the last chapter, is to fully understand and embrace the *'privilege'* aspect of caregiving.

Third: Unselfish Love.

'Unselfish love' is the *'third rail,'* the one down the center between *'commitment'* and *'endurance.'* Unselfish love supplies the *'inexhaustible power'* we need to survive, thrive and embrace the privilege of caregiving. I believe the well of unselfish love comes directly from God via our soul, as we become *'soul driven.'*

The Bond of Friendship.

Friendship is a fruit of unselfish love. To have a friend we need to be a friend. A simple thought but true. As caregivers we need to take the time to reach out and develop a network of friends. As supporters of caregivers, we need to put our insecurities aside and reach out to them. Don't wait for an invitation. They don't want pity or a lot of attention. It just helps to know someone cares.

> "The highest proof of the Spirit is love.
> Love is the eternal thing which men can
> already on earth possess as it really is."
>
> — Albert Schweitzer

Making Good Choices:

Here is some good news. As caregivers we are not totally out of control. There are other choices we can make that will chart our course as we deal with the wild ride ahead.

We 'Grew Up' with Jessica

Good Choices: Find Your Perspective.

Keeping our eye on the prize is to keep the proper perspective. We are choosing to live in the world of the caregiver. We need to see the big picture and at the same time, stay focused in the present. All we have is today, so we need to make the most of it and have no fear of the future. One day, one hour or one minute at a time.

Good Choices: Character.

Character is right in our wheelhouse. It is the rudder we use to set and hold our course. It is acquired over time as we use our navigational charts of *'commitment,' 'endurance'* and *'unselfish love,'* to face the storms. As we make good choices and keep our eyes on the purpose of our mission, our character grows.

Good character is the habit of good choices. Unselfish love does make it easier to make good choices.

The Fruits of Our Labors.

Staying on course we begin to see the fruit of our labors. The sooner we begin, and the quicker we yield our self will, the faster things may happen. Sometimes delays happen, but a *'delay is not a defeat,'* as old Albert would say. Our patience has a chance to grow. Our character is strengthened by adversity.

Confidence, Hope & Patience.

As we stay the course and see a steady progression in our ability to cope, our confidence grows. We learn to take off and fly. We learn the lesson of being patient, that delay is not defeat, and then the

Lessons from JESSICA

miracle of hope invigorates us, and a hopeful vision of the future motivates us. And we realize that with resolve, we can do this.

> "I can do things you cannot, you can do things I cannot; together we can do great things."
>
> Mother Teresa

Blessings, Joy & Faith.

The three touchstones of a *'soul driven'* life are a life lived with purpose, love and care this is the privileged role of the *'caregiver.'*

I always remember the lesson of the farmer. They prepare, they plant, they feed, nourish and care, as they wait patiently for the harvest. The *growth* they seek comes from their *faith*. And then when harvest time is here, come bountiful *blessings* and *joy*.

Faith unlocks the door to ultimate caregiving, blessings & joy.

Future Joy.

In my mind's eye I can look forward to strolling the blooming fields of heaven, walking hand in hand with my family and listening to Jessica giggle like a bubbling brook, as we recount our lives together as we *'grew up'* in love at the Walker house.

And she will turn to me and say *"I love you Dad, I have always loved you."* And then we will go and find a very big piano.

"Absolutely!"

We are privileged to live in *'JessicaLand.'* We do not labor in vain.

Study & Discussion QUESTIONS.

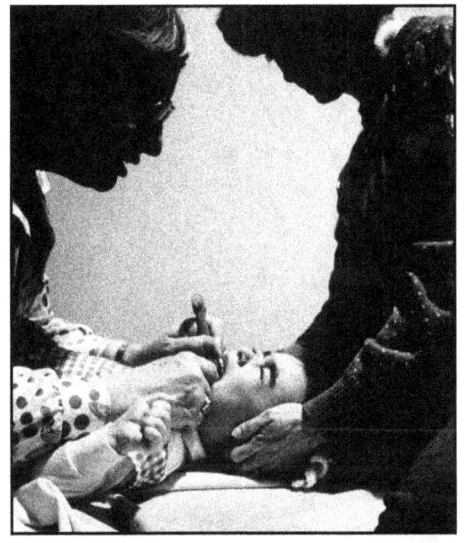

Arnold Gold Photo   1984

Understanding Ultimate Caregiving.

Lessons from JESSICA

Understanding Ultimate Caregiving

Chapter 19

Study & Discussion Questions.

Understanding Ultimate Caregiving.

This chapter contains a collection of highlighted questions and comments, for your consideration and discussion. The purpose is to encapsulate the concepts I have presented and to hopefully spark your thinking & further facilitate *'ultimate caregiving.*

Primary Caregivers, Secondary Caregivers, Friends of Caregivers, and anyone who *observes caregiving activities* will find this information helpful and supportive in paving the way to embracing the privileges and blessings of caregiving.

Study Questions for Review by Chapter.

> **CHAPTER ONE**
> *Into the* UNDISCOVERED LAND
> *What is 'Ultimate Caregiving?'*

How many estimated caregivers are in the USA? (p.23) How many caregivers do you know? Are you a caregiver? Why?

What is 'ultimate caregiving?' What kind of choices are needed? (p.24) What are the 4 types of caregivers? (p.25) Which type are you? How do you feel about caregiving?

Who was Dr. Viktor Frankel? (p.26) What helped Viktor make his decision? What kind of love did he choose? (p28)

Lessons from JESSICA

Why is everyone's journey both different and the same? (p.29)

> **CHAPTER TWO**
> *Your PROBLEMS or MINE?*
> *A Matter of Perspective.*

Why is 'perspective' important? (p.34) What is a secret of coping with affliction and caregiving? (p.35) Why?

What are the threads of *'ultimate caregiving?'* (p.36) What is the first thing you will need, that is a part of every other good thing? (p.37)

> **CHAPTER THREE**
> *The Glue of COMMITMENT.*
> *A Really, Really Long Word.*

Why is 'commitment' the word without an end? What two things does it require? Why are they hard decisions? (p.41)

As caregivers how often is our commitment tested? (p.42)

If you are committed how does that affect your *'free will?'* What kind of a commitment is needed? How long does this kind of commitment last? (p.43) Why?

What is the first fruit of this kind of commitment? (p.44)

What special kind of love adds dimensions to your commitment? (p.44) Why?

CHAPTER FOUR
ENDURANCE for the RACE.
Sprint or Marathon?

What kind of a 'gap' does 'endurance' bridge? (p.48) Why?

What are 'small acts of kindness?' What happens when we put our love and concern into action? (p.49)

Why do we sometimes 'freeze up' when we are around caregivers and receivers? What is the importance of perspective? When should you commit a small act of kindness? (p.50)

Should you wait until they ask for help? Why or why not?

What's the heart and soul of commitment & endurance? (p.51)

What can you do when you feel like quitting? (p.52)

CHAPTER FIVE
A LOVE that is GENUINE.
Acquiring Unselfishness.

What kind of love did little Agnes embrace? (p.56)

What does unselfish love say? Of what, does 'unselfish love' consist? Why is that important? (p.56)

What are the 'three rails' on the 'caregiving rollercoaster?' (p.60)

Viktor, Agnes and Josh are examples of the power of 'ultimate love.' Why is that a critical factor in 'ultimate caregiving?' (p.61)

Lessons from JESSICA

> **CHAPTER SIX**
> *Make Lasting FRIENDSHIPS.*
> *The Fruits of Unselfish Love.*

What are 'genuine friendships?' Why are they important? Why should you not be afraid to befriend a caregiver? Why is it enough to be a caring friend? (p.66)

What is the focus of a caregiver? Should caregivers continue to reach out for friendship? Are you afraid of their friendship? Why or why not? (p.67) Do you think you can make a difference? Why or why not?

What is the purpose of 'Lessons from Jessica?' Why should caregivers make their needs known? Do you see the blessings and privileges of caregiving? (p.68)

> **CHAPTER SEVEN**
> *Keeping Your PERSPECTIVE.*
> *The Width, Breadth & Depth of Life.*

What is the 'power of perspective?' Have you experienced a 'paradigm shift'? (p.72)

How does 'perspective' affect caregiving? Why is it important to have an optimistic perspective for the future? (p.73)

As a caregiver, is it possible to be 'optimistic?' Can you be joyful with a broken heart? Why or why not? (p.74)

Define free will. What is the impact of 'free will' choices on our perspective? (p.74) Has it made a difference to you?

Understanding Ultimate Caregiving

> **CHAPTER EIGHT**
> *Developing CHARACTER*
> *More than a Cartoon.*

How does 'character' help? Where does it come from? What is the best foundation for our character? (p.78)

Does 'good character' just happen? Does 'bad character' just happen? (p.79)

How did Albert's good, strong character, commitment and endurance change the world for the better? (p.80)

Can we change for the better and grow into a better person through the experience of caregiving? What happens when we begin to see caregiving as a privilege? (p.81)

What can keep us on a truer course? (p.81)

> **CHAPTER NINE**
> *Growing CONFIDENCE.*
> *Trust in your Future.*

What is 'confidence' a big part of? What exercises help us develop more confidence? (p.85)

What is 'faith?' What is the 'good news?' What does history show about the caregiving path? (p.87)

Can you see the privilege in 'caregiving?' Why or why not? Do you have confidence in your future as a caregiver? Why?

Lessons from JESSICA

> **CHAPTER TEN**
> *The Miracle of HOPE.*
> *Confidence Breeds Hope.*

What is 'hope?' What is 'hopelessness?' (p.92)

What are the choices we control that are a part of hope? What are the long term benefits of our positive choices? (p.93)

> **CHAPTER ELEVEN**
> *Where is My PATIENCE?*
> *Running Out of It?*

What is patience? (p.97)

How was Helen's soul emancipated? (p.98)

What is the characteristic of unselfish love? (p.99) Why?

> **CHAPTER TWELVE**
> *The Fruit of BLESSINGS*
> *Flowing From Sacrifice.*

What wonderful fruit does caregiving produce in our lives? Why does that happen? How long can it take? (p.105)

What does Helen say about the best and most beautiful things in our lives? (p.106)

Do you see how the principles of ultimate caregiving can work for anyone? Can you see how sorrow turns into joy? (p.107)

Understanding Ultimate Caregiving

CHAPTER THIRTEEN
Amazing JOY.
Adding Everything Up.

Can you see how God is the 'ultimate caregiver?' Can you have joy and a broken heart? What should be our motivation and purpose in our caregiving? (p.105) Why or why not?

What is real 'joy' like? What is joy not? (p.114)

What is the critical power source for our joy? (p.115)

What are some key ingredients we need to find the joy and blessings on the path to ultimate caregiving? (p.116)

CHAPTER FOURTEEN
Considering FAITH.
Someone is at The Door.

What allowed us to learn our 'lessons from Jessica?' Where does 'ultimate caregiving' lead us? (p.122)

Where can you find help if you have doubts? (p.123)

CHAPTER FIFTEEN
Help for HELPLESS.
Who is the Helpless One?

What were the three things I learned in my hospital experience? (p.105)

What is the definition of a grateful heart? (p.130)

Lessons from JESSICA

Have you ever been helpless and under the care of others? How did that make you feel? What did you learn from that?

Where should our focus as a caregivers be? Do you feel 'privileged' or 'enslaved?' Why or why not? (p.131)

If the person you provide caregiving for could read your mind how would that change your perspective? (p.132)

CHAPTER SIXTEEN
Consider the SOUL.
What is a Soul Worth?

From a personal perspective would you agree that 'our life is in our memories?' Why or why not. What is our dwelling place? What are some of our bodies characteristics? (p.135)

Where do our thoughts live? How many conscious thoughts can we have at any given instant? How is that an asset? (p.136)

How hard is 'self-love?' What are the inborn physical appetites that 'self love' is focused on? Why? (p.136)

How important is the 'soul?' What are the three choices we have in life? Which choice supports ultimate caregiving? (p.137)

How valuable is the human soul? I believe that the 'soul' is the well of eternity. Does that make sense to you? Why or why not? What choices do we control? What are the long term benefits of those choices? (p.141)

Understanding Ultimate Caregiving

CHAPTER SEVENTEEN
It is Our PRIVILEGE.
The Greatest of them All.

What kind of privilege are we talking about here? How important is embracing our role and understanding the significance of our mission? (p.145)

Why does understanding our 'great privilege' as caregivers lead to ultimate victory and peace of mind?(p.145)

What is deep inspiration? As caregivers what great privilege have we been given? Why is it important to understand that principle? What is 'God's perspective?'(p.148)

What are the three things that Helen thanked God for every day of her life? (p.149)

CHAPTER EIGHTEEN
Traveling in JESSICA-LAND.
We 'Grew Up' with Jessica.

Have the principles shared in this book been helpful to you? Can you see the benefit of learning and applying the information I have shared? (p.154)

As a 'Primary Caregiver,' to what do you need to be totally committed? How important is 'endurance?' (p.155)

How important is 'unselfish love' to caregiving? What is a fruit of unselfish love? What do we need to put aside? Why? (p.156)

Lessons from JESSICA

How important is a proper perspective? Why? How is character acquired over time? How does unselfish love help? Why is it important to have *'commitment,' 'endurance,' & 'unselfishness?'* Why would Albert say *'delay is not defeat?'* (p.157)

How important are confidence, hope and patience? What did Agnes say we could do together? What are the three touchstones of a *'soul-driven'* life? What door does faith unlock? (p.158)

No matter what our circumstances, how can we all confidently look forward to future joy?

> **SUGGESTED ACTIVITIES**
> **to SUPPORT and ENCOURAGE**
> **the CAREGIVERS in your life.**

For suggested activities, resources and materials for growth and support of *'ultimate caregivers'* see the *'Caregiver Resource'* section in the *Appendix* that follows. (p 171)

You may want to take the *'12 days of Hope Challenge'.* (p175)

The challenge is to send a card or note of encouragement to the *'caregivers'* in your life. Not an *'e-mail'* or any other electronic signal, but a *real live handwritten note* from you to them.

APPENDIX

1984

Books, Resources, & References.

Lessons from JESSICA

Chapter 20

APPENDIX

Books, Resources & References.

TABLE OF CONTENTS:

Resources for Caregiving:	175
'The 12 days of Hope Challenge.'	175
Your Review Requested	176
Chart of Quotes:	177

> Viktor
> Vince
> Agnes
> Josh
> Albert
> Anne
> Helen
> Jesus
> The Bible.

Books by Josh McDowell:	179

> *More Than a Carpenter*
> *The NEW Evidence That Demands a Verdict.*
> *God Breathed*

Lessons from JESSICA

Websites and Digital Resources: 181
    Bible App
    Josh.org
    GreatnewsPress.com

GreatNewsPress.com Inspirational Books: 182
    Growing Up with Jessica: A True Story
    Lessons from Jessica: Ultimate Caregiving

Photojournalist Arnold Gold   185

Summary Bibliography: 187

Personal Note Pages: 191

APPENDIX

Resources for Caregiving.

The '12 Days of Hope' Challenge.

As I created this book I kept thinking of a way to lower the bar for those that want to get onboard as a *'caregiver supporter.'*

In looking back over the years, one of the things that our family found ourselves treasuring, were the simple handwritten notes and cards of support we received. I know it is a little old fashioned, but it fits the *'...small things with great love...'* description perfectly.

My challenge to you is to send 12 cards to the caregivers in your life with a little handwritten note inside. It can brighten their day. Sending just one per month takes but a moment, and you are creating treasure for their soul. Who knows... you may be the difference for your special caregiver. A bright beam of light on a dark and gloomy day. It is a simple act that can lead to a loving friendship. Friendship can open the path to love and support.

Many opportunities may come your way through a simple act of kindness. Sending a card is a simple act of love that anyone can do. Who knows where it can lead. Take the challenge and you will see.

Your love can make a difference if you put it into action. Always remember that unselfish love is *'love in action.'*

I really believe that if you do this 12 times and see the results, you will be blessed. You will be a part of God's 'ultimate caregiving.'

Your Review Requested

Your Review Matters:

Thank You for Reading this Caregiver's Guide!

I know your time is valuable and I do appreciate you investing it in this book. I have shared from my heart our story in the hope that you would be encouraged and inspired by our true life affliction, our struggles and the joy and victory we are now experiencing. I hope you have a deeper understanding of caregiving and that the lessons I have shared in this 'caregiver's guide' will offer comfort, support, and inspiration, to you and your family and friends.

Your Opinion is Critical to 'Ultimate Caregiving.'

Our readers usually respond with a desire for others to read this 'Caregiver's Guide.' One of the most effective ways to achieve the goal of sharing your experience, is reviewing the book at online retailers like: **Amazon.com, BarnesandNoble.com, or iBooks.**

Also helpful are book fan websites like: **www.Goodreads.com**

Your opinion does matter and it really is crucial to the ongoing exposure of this book. Please reference these ISBN numbers:

'Growing Up with Jessica: A True Story.'
Blessed by the Unexpected Parenting of a Special Needs Child.

Print-ISBN 978-0-9800641-0-0
eBook-ISBN 9780980064124
Apple iBook-ISBN 9780980064148

'Lessons from Jessica: Ultimate Caregiving.'
A Longtime Caregiver's Inspirational Guide to Understanding and Ultimately Succeeding at Caregiving.

Print-ISBN: 978-1-944080-00-6
eBook-ISBN 9781944080013

To share your Caregiver Story: jessicabookboise@gmail.com

Books, Resources & References

Chart of Quotes:

Quotes in the order of appearance:

Viktor Frankel	p.27, p.28, p.48, p.61, p.91, p.138
Vince Lombardi	p.43
Agnes Bojaxhiu	p.55-56, p.57, p.61, p.66, p.73, p.106 p.148, p.158
Josh McDowell	p.59, p.61, p.120, p.138
Albert Schweitzer	p.80, p.81, p.86, p.156, p.157
Anne Sullivan	p.98, p.139
Helen Keller	p.98-99, p.140, p.149, p.155
Jesus Christ	p.113, p.123, p.141
The Bible	p.113, p.121

FOOTNOTE:

(1) According to the The National Alliance for Caregiving & AARP Caregiving in the U.S. National Alliance for Caregiving, Washington, D.C. '65.7 million informal and formal caregivers provide care to someone who is ill, diabled or aged in the U.S.'

Lessons from JESSICA

Books, Resources & References

APPENDIX

Personal Resources

Books by Josh McDowell

About Josh McDowell:

To say that Josh has had a huge impact on Renée and I and our faith would be an understatement. Josh the skeptic, thought that Christians were out of their minds. He ridiculed and insulted them, then decided to disprove the claims of Jesus Christ. To his surprise he discoverd that the evidence suggested exactly the opposite...that Jesus, instead of being simply a first-century Hebrew carpenter, truly was the God he claimed to be.

Since that day in 1959 he has become what I consider to be the foremost defender of Christianity alive today. Author of over 140 books, Josh has spoken to over 25 million people in 125 countries, including over 700 university and college campuses.

For more information & resources see his website at: www.josh.org

More Than a Carpenter
ISBN 978-1-4143-2627-6

Over 15 million copies in print since it's original publication, *More Than a Carpenter* has changed countless lives. Now in this revised and updated edition, Josh is joined by his son, Sean, as they tackle the questions that today's generation continues to ask. A very readable and understandable book.

Tyndale Publishing, 180 pages

Lessons from JESSICA

The NEW Evidence That Demands a Verdict
ISBN 978-0-78524-363-2

Christians today face growing challenges to show that their faith is both relevant and credible. This book combines the two original best-selling *Evidence that Demands a Verdict* volumes into one, maintaining their classic defense of Christianity, yet at the same time answering new questions posed by today's culture. This is a great in-depth book for those honestly seeking evidence to believe or defend the faith. An amazing resource.

Thomas Nelson Publishers, 760 pages

GOD Breathed
ISBN 978-1-63058-941-7

Join Josh as he provides clear evidence that God's Word is living, relevant, reliable and historically trustwothy. Sharing his own story as a 'skeptic turned believer,' and his recently acquired, 'never seen before' ancient scriptural artifacts.

Recapture the awe, the mystery, the passion and the power of Christian scripture.

Shiloh Run Press, 216 pages.

APPENDIX

Websites & Digital Resources

Life's Deeper Questions & Answers.

Of course in this digital age, there are always digital forms and resources to choose from. Most can be accessed via all of your devices at anytime. The ones listed here are free.

'YouVersion Bible App' address: *http://bible.com/app*

This is an extremely helpful and beneficial app that you can download to any device. This app by *Life Church*, called simply *'Bible,'* offers an abundance of educational materials for your own Bible references and studies. Very convenient and efficient.

'Bible' app offers hundreds of Bible versions in many different languages, some audio versions too. The Bible app also offers Bible study plans on many different topics. You can also highlight and personalize. Includes a 'search' feature. Downloaded by millions.

Josh McDowell Website address: *www.josh.org*

This site gives you access to a multitude of resources and references including digital versions of many books by Josh McDowell & his son Sean. Includes their biographical backgrounds and topical studies. Worth checking out.

GreatNewsPress.com Website: *www.GreatNewsPress.com*

This site specializes in inspirational books like this one.

Lessons from JESSICA

The Books in the 'Growing Up with Jessica' Series:
Christian Choice Book Awards, DOUBLE Winner:

'First Place'
'Best Parenting Book'
and one of three
'Grand Prize'
Winners.

Growing Up with Jessica: A True Story
Blessed by the Unexpected Parenting of a Special Needs Child.

Print: ISBN 978-0-9800641-0-0
eBook: ISBN 9780980064124
Apple iBook: ISBN 9780980064148

This award winning true story, told clearly and passionately by Jessica's father is moving as well as inspiring

Shaken to the very roots of their faith, they found understanding and ultimate victory as they *'grew up'* as the unexpected caregivers for Jessica.

Paperback 200 pages

A very touching and inspiring adventure that is part mystery, part tragedy, and 100% inspirational. It will take you on an emotional roller coaster ride through tragedy, love, faith, hope and blessings. You will finally emerge, touched and inspired, with a *'full heart.'*

> "I encourage you to read this book because it will touch you, minister to you and my hope is that you will conclude, as I did, that you will become a better person and parent as the result..."
>
> Josh McDowell, Author & Speaker

Books, Resources & References

Lessons from Jessica: Ultimate Caregiving.
A Longtime Caregiver's Inspirational Guide to Understanding and Ultimately Succeeding at Caregiving.

Print: ISBN: 978-1-944080-00-6 (196 pp)
eBook: ISBN: 9781944080013

From James Walker, the *Award Winning Author* and Jessica's Dad.

Walker recounts the lessons learned and truths revealed over nearly 40 years as a 24/7 caregiver. Practical time-tested principles found in this 'caregivers guide' does show clearly the path to ultimate success.

Written to raise awareness, understanding, and support for *'caregivers, their families, friends and observers.'* He shares how to breakthrough, highlighting successful concepts and the *'ultimate privilege'* of providing the life-giving care, for another human soul.

Explained are practical ways to acquire the commitment, endurance, and unselfish love needed to become what he describes as an *'ultimate caregiver.'* Other topics include, the importance of friendships, personal character development, confidence, the miracle of hope, understanding patience, finding blessings, amazing joy and faith, understanding helplessness, the worth of the human soul, and the privilege of caregiving, all of which adds up to the *'ultimate caregiving'* experience.

He also weaves into his narrative, insights from the lives of *Viktor Frankel, Mother Teresa, Albert Schweitzer, Ann Sullivan, Helen Keller, Josh McDowell & Jesus Christ*, along with his own practical life experiences. And also includes simple and practical ways to offer support and encouragement. Anyone reading Walker's book will be encouraged and inspired by his guide to *'ultimate caregiving.'*

Lessons from JESSICA

Books, Resources & References

APPENDIX

Credits, Photo Notes & Bibliography

Resources & References

Arnold Gold, Photojournalist.

I answered the door and there stood a nervous young man loaded down with cameras. *"You must be Arnold Gold,"* I said as I reached to shake his hand, *"Come in we are ready for you."*

Thus began another little amazing adventure in 'Jessica-land.'

Somehow Arnold's first assignment was to be a human interest story about our daughter Jessica. He had recently graduated from Syracuse University and was in Boise doing a student internship with our local paper. To this day I am not sure why he was given the assignment, or even how the assignment began. The year was 1984.

He was a very polite and intelligent young man, and I could see his sensitivity as he gently probed us, asking questions about Jessica. We really hit it off right away and the best was yet to come.

Arnold had positioned himself in the room with the adroit instincts of a photo artist. Renée brought Jessica into the room and laid her on a bright comforter on the floor at his feet.

Jessica looked straight into the camera and immediately broke into a beautiful dimpled smile of delight...'click' went the camera and Arnold, who had traveled so far to be with us that day, captured on film the first, really spontaneous smile, we had ever seen from Jessica.

Lessons from JESSICA

To say that we were stunned would be an understatement.

It was one of those very sweet and special moments that defy explanation. It is a photo that we still treasure.

The shot ran in full color, with Arnold's story, in the newspaper a few days later. For years after, we would be in the hospital, or a lab, or doctor's waiting room, or even in line at the grocery story and people would recognize Jessica. The story and photo was so well received that Arnold returned and did a much more in depth story.

He followed us a round that summer and took many more photos. He did a 2 page spread in the paper entitled, *'Jessica, the Blessed One.'* For his efforts, Arnold received a national award from the National Press Photographers Association in 1984.

When I was working on my first book, **Growing Up with Jessica**, I was looking at the copies of the photos he had given us and the newspaper clippings from that time together 20 years before. I got on the internet and after a few tries found Arnold's website. He was amazed, and so was I, when I found out he had only had a website for about a week. Just another Jessica-land experience.

I tried to use as many of Arnold's photo in this book as I could, you will note Arnold Gold's name in the lower left corner. As for the 'smiling Jessica' photo, you will find it on the back cover.

> *"...As I have a daughter now, I understand more intimately, the vunerability in their being, and so Jessica's story touches me on a different level..."*
>
> Arnold Gold, 2004
> *www.arnoldgold.com*

Thank you Arnold, for coming into our lives and blessing us with your incredibly sensitive photography. We will never forget you!

Books, Resources & References

Notes about Bibliographical Information and Sources:

Here is a brief overview of my sources and general documentation for the individual biographies studied and quoted in this book.

All of the writing in *'Lessons from Jessica: Ultimate Caregiving,'* about the named individuals below, unless a direct quote, is the creation and intelllectual property of James Walker, the author of this work, and may be used with permission if credited.

GreatNewsPress.com, Publisher
James Walker, Author

Individuals or Sources Quoted in this Book:

The individual biographies in both printed form, and as offered on-line, were used to document and check the accuracy of their lives and statements, and used to prepare this publication. This included but was not limited to, a combination of their *'official'* websites if existant, and other information which is a matter of public record. Every attempt was made to crosscheck for accuracy.

Agnes Gonxhe Bojaxhiu (Mother Teresa)(1910-1997)
Albert Schweitzer (1875-1965)
Anne Sullivan (1866-1936)
Helen Keller (1880-1968)
Josh McDowell (1939)
Viktor Frankel (1905-1997)
Vince Lombardi (1913-1970)
Jesus Christ
The Bible

Lessons from JESSICA

APPENDIX

Growing Up with Jessica

A Joyful Blessing.

Renée and I have been blessed in many ways since my first book was published in 2004-5. Our sometimes comical adventures have continued, as we *'make our mark... wherever we go!'*

We have walked the 2000 year-old cobblestones at Edinburgh Castle in Scotland. I have played golf at both the St. Andrews and Turnberry courses over there. I even brought back some sand.

We have sailed the Caribbean with Jessica and our family, on the largest cruise ship in the world. We have strolled the beaches in Koolini, Hawaii three separate times. The last time with our life long friends joining us. We have spent quality time with Mickey & Minnie, with our grandkids in tow, a number of times.

Renee & Jim with our grandkids at Redfish Lake, Idaho in 2013.
From left; Jacob, Benjamin, Emerson & Elijah.

Lessons from JESSICA

We have prayed in Billy Graham' prayer chapel and church in North, Carolina, and even left them a copy of *'Growing Up with Jessica'* for their library. A beautiful and serene memory.

We have shared a chicken pot pie in the cozy pub at the Vanderbilt Estate, while sitting by the warm fire and recounting our blessings, while the rain poured down outside. A joyful experience.

We have been evacuated from several luxury hotels by false alarms. Once getting lost in the basement laundry room at the Disney Hawaiian Aulani Resort. I remember shining my flashlight in the laundry bin and seeing Mickey and Minnie's clothes in there!

We have traveled far, and the road extends before us into infinity and beyond! Our hearts are broken but we are surviving and thriving and experiencing the joy and peace that only God knows.

We are watching our kids and grandkids grow up in the lovely grandeur that we call Idaho. Indian legend says that *'Ee-dow-how'* is a word meaning *'sun shining on the mountains.'* And I am reminded that the sun is always shining, no matter how big the mountain before us. In fact you could say the bigger the mountain the more sun it reflects. A comforting thought as we grow older.

It is my sincere prayer, that this little book makes a positive difference for you and yours. I truly believe that if you examine the principles I have outlined it will be helpful and make your path easier. I am convinced because I am experiencing it everyday.

May God bless all of the caregivers in every way possible. You and I can make a difference. Remember, unselfish love *is* love in action.

James Walker

Your Personal Notespace:

Lessons from JESSICA

Your Personal Notespace:

Lessons from JESSICA

www.ingramcontent.com/pod-product-compliance
Lightning Source LLC
Chambersburg PA
CBHW071617080526
44588CB00010B/1165